THE DEATH OF
RETIREMENT

Breaking Your Reliance on a Broken
System by Investing in Cash Engines

DAVID SCHNEIDER

THE
WRITINGALE
PUBLISHING

DAVID SCHNEIDER

The Writingale Publishing also publishes its books in a variety of electronic formats. For more information about The Writingale Publishing products, visit our Web site at www.thewritingale.com.

ISBN-13: 978-1975633868
ISBN-10: 1975633865

Printed in the United States of America
First Edition: September 2017
10 9 8 7 6 5 4 3 2 1

.

Investing for retirement is a daunting task, and just reading a book without pursuing further experience and information will be insufficient to achieve fundamental change in your investment approach.

To encourage positive action for those who are committed to studying investing, and to continuously provide motivation and inspiration to develop and improve your personal investment approach, I have set up a members-only website. The members' area will provide additional learning resources for some of the observations in this book and all my other investing publications.

Here are just a few of the resources which come with the membership:

- Accompanying graphs, charts and tables
- Checklists and case studies
- Access to our 8020 Model Portfolio
- Access to an exclusive Facebook group where we discuss investment ideas and recent investment trends
- And more...

To claim your FREE membership, go to:

www.super8020.com/free-member

I recommend to post your questions or comments about any topic covered in this book in our dedicated forum, or exclusive Facebook Group. Discuss your ideas or concerns with other like-minded investors. Gain insights into the world of investing, and begin your journey to financial freedom. I wish you all success on your investing journey and thanks for reading

David Schneider

Cuiusvis hominis est errare,
nullius nisi insipientis in errore perseverare

~Cicero

CONTENTS

ACKNOWLEDGMENTS

I would like to extend my thanks to John Cavendish, Miles Beckler and Travis Jamison for their patience and the vivid stories they provided me with for this book. They are a true inspiration for a new generation of enlightened investors. Special thanks goes to my launch team and all the people who reviewed and critiqued this book. My editor, Subodhana Wijeyeratne, has been a great help in formulating some general arguments on a complex topic—and undoubtedly has put his stamp on this piece of work. His wealth of historical knowledge has been extremely helpful in identifying some of the trends discussed here. Valerie Smith, is the critical voice and eye of the team. I thank her for her time and unflagging patience. Both are very talented writers, whom I highly recommend. I am grateful to my production team, which encompasses designers, guests, proofreaders, and many more. I would like to thank my numerous friends from the DC community, my mastermind groups, as well as my sources and contacts in the financial industry who have always offered a helping hand whenever I needed it. As always, I am grateful to my parents. They gave me all the opportunities a son could wish for, which has allowed me to explore the world.

THE DEATH OF RETIREMENT

INTRODUCTION

What if I told you that everything you knew about investing for retirement was wrong?

What if I told you that what we call 'investing' these days is just millions of people over the world being lured into a game they don't understand?

We are all conditioned to think about the world of finance, stocks markets, and mutual fund products as an easy route to riches, and even more so when it comes to saving for retirement. More often than not, we're told that the only real way to grow your pot of cash is through investing in financial markets.

However, this book will show that idea is completely wrong. Investing in financial markets for retirement is nothing more than a fool's game evolved over decades of relative prosperity in a few countries.

If what Taylor Pearson (author of *The End of Jobs*) and James Altucher (author of *Choose Yourself*)[1] say is even remotely true, this has very serious consequences for all of us. All these authors and others make strong cases that the traditional route to retirement is bust, and that we are in for some fundamental changes over the next 20 to 30 years—changes that will have a devastating effect on how we all have to save and invest for our future.

Yet, instead of coming up with valid alternatives and new approaches to retirement, most mainstream advisors recommend more of the same: 'financial product variation,' expensive financial 'advice,' and elaborate 'diversification' models. What I find most horrifying about this is how early in their lives people are lured into these flawed systems and how completely people believe that these systems are the only way to secure their future.

In the following pages, we will take a brief look at the conventional approach to investing for retirement; its flaws, and consequences. In part one, we will look at how the contemporary investment system is failing. We will look at why we, as investors, often end up at the losing end of a grant bet that is called retirement. We'll also see how the industry manipulates us into handing over our money, though their interests are not necessarily the same as ours. In the second part, we will look at how we *should* approach investing for retirement and what we actually should be investing in—independent of what financial literature or vested interests suggest. We will explore an approach that is more in tune with real economics, value creation, and most importantly, with hardworking, middle-income folk with priorities beyond simply buying and selling slices of other people's pies. You will be shown how to avoid blindly following platitudes, and how to understand today's financial markets and to invest in a context that is more suitable to our own shortcomings and cognitive biases.

We will also explore how you could make use of flaws for your benefit.

If we ever want to free ourselves from the current vicious cycle of financial disappointments and dependency on the same retirement platitudes, we need to understand and overcome the current system and approach to retirement investing. That is the goal of this book.

DAVID SCHNEIDER

PART I:
CONVENTIONAL RETIREMENT INVESTING

CHAPTER 1
FAILURE OF PENSIONS

Here is a basic definition of what a pension is:

> "A pension is a fund into which a sum of money is added during an employee's employment years, and from which payments are drawn to support the person's retirement from work in the form of periodic payments."[2]

Not too long ago, large numbers of Americans enjoyed a pension dream world. Traditional pensions guaranteed a steady stream of payments until the recipient's death. Known as "defined benefit plans," the payouts were set and predetermined in advance. Together with the benefits of Social Security, the average worker enjoyed a robust safety net.

This system was not that old. The Social Security Act was passed only in 1935, and as late as 1940, only 12 % of workers had pensions. By 1975, just 55.2%—that is, little more than half—of all American workers were covered by pensions. This growth was driven by unprecedented prosperity, where the US particularly saw a post-World War 2 boom.

But today's pension and social security reality looks very different, and there is no better example than the story of CalPERS, the California Public Employees' Retirement System (CalPERS). CalPERS is the largest state pension fund in the US, and "manages pension and health benefits for more than 1.6

DAVID SCHNEIDER

million California public employees, retirees, and their families."[3]According to *Fortune Magazine*, "the fund has 68 cents in assets for every dollar in liabilities, assuming that it continues to earn returns of 7.5% per year, though it has failed to do that for two years in a row." Those words were published in June 2016 and 2017 doesn't look any better. *Fortune* traces the problem back to "a combination of an aging population, tight state budgets, and an unwillingness on the part of politicians to force public sector unions or taxpayers to contribute more to these pension funds.[4] In fact, *most* pension plans in the US and around the world are technically and practically broke. Municipal bankruptcies are increasing in the US as their pension obligations balloon. Many traditional industries such as steel and airlines have already rid themselves of pension obligations by declaring Chapter 11 bankruptcy.

[i] Traditional pensions are underfunded by trillions of dollars.[4] As mutual fund expert William Birdthistle put it, "The golden age of the pension…is effectively over."[5]

The situation for Social Security doesn't look better. The average monthly benefit for retirees from Social Security in the US is now $1,335, or just over $16,000 per year.[3] Imagine trying to survive on just over $1000 a month at the age of 70, with healthcare bills, food, rent, and other necessities. Not a pretty picture, is it?

Forced to Flirt with Risk

One way of getting around this shortfall is for big pension-providing institutions to invest in volatile assets. This is what the Government Pension Investment Fund (GPIF) of Japan (the biggest pension fund in the world, with $1.1 trillion in assets under management) did.

For most of its life, the GPIF was famous for having an ultra-conservative investment policy, keeping almost 60% of its assets in

---

[i] a form of controlled bankruptcy

2

risk-free domestic fixed income securities, and 11% in high-grade international bonds—with slim investments to domestic and international stocks. That changed in October 2014.

The GPIF (and, in fact, many other pension funds around the world) concluded that there was only one way to compensate for the complete collapse of interest income in today's new low-interest regime: investing more in stocks and other risky assets managed by third parties. The GPIF increased allocation to domestic and international stocks to 50% of their portfolios. People argued that their whole reason for existence is "to provide retirement income security for the remaining life of the plan member;"[6] if they didn't do something to ensure that, weren't they being negligent in their duties?

Because their own investment management team was not equipped to handle such a large allocation of stocks, the GPIF had to hire over thirty advisory firms. The list of who the GPIF turned to reads like the who's who of money management—firms such as Fidelity, Morgan Stanley, and Goldman Sachs.

For them, it was a fee bonanza, and it was one that didn't end there. The bandwagon effect, where people primarily do something just because others are doing it regardless of their own beliefs, is a very strong one in Japan, and in rapid succession most major pension funds in Japan followed suit, converting their ultra-conservative investment policies into higher-powered equity portfolios with professional asset managers. Hence, the risk situation abruptly changed for the GPIF and for the many Japanese pension funds following the GPIF's lead.

Soon enough, the GPIF, and the people who rely on it for their pensions got their first bitter taste of market volatility when the GPIF reported a massive paper loss of ¥5.3tn ($52.8bn, a loss of 3.88%) in the 2nd quarter of 2016. Their money had just vanished into thin air. It was one of the biggest losses in the entire history of the GPIF.

The GPIF's experience is just the tip of the iceberg. Exposure to unpredictable, and at times extremely volatile high-risk capital gains, can have severe financial consequences. In 2008, for example, private pensions lost a staggering $5.4 trillion—nearly a quarter of their value.[7] And in case you were wondering, this is not a pathology unique to pensions. In September 2016, the famed Harvard Management Company announced it had lost almost $2 billion in endowment value during the "disappointing" fiscal year 2016, its worst endowment returns since the nadir of the financial crisis.[8]

While government and corporate pension plans could buffer against the wider shocks and some of the skullduggeries by Wall Street, due to their sheer size and professional organizational structures, individuals managing their retirement by themselves have less of that luxury. Worse, they, as individuals, seem to be less equipped to cope with the psychological side-effects modern capital market investing has on them. Unfortunately, there is an irreversible process going on that has put more and more responsibility on the individual, forcing them to fend for themselves and their retirement away from traditional pensions and social security. As we shall see, the argument is that with big pension-providing institutions failing, as described above, we're all better off taking care of our own retirement. Unfortunately, it's not quite working out that way, as we'll see below.

Demographics and Prediction: The Twin Terrors

In the case of social security, a rapidly aging society and demographic shifts are mentioned as the main reasons why we shouldn't expect full benefit payments down the road. The concept of social security is based on contributions by the younger generations to support older ones; the young, in turn, will expect to be supported by *their* children when *they* grow up and become taxpayers. Crucially, *it is not actually based on what people in the past paid into the system*, because that is not nearly enough. As a result, some experts have even called it a giant Ponzi scheme. It's only natural that the system cannot sustain itself if the generations that follow are much smaller than the generation that preceded them—as it will be in many countries where the baby boomer generation is about to retire.

What makes the task of managing any pension so challenging are the questions of how long we will live and how much we will be spending on medical bills. Add unpredictable financial markets and tax and inflation uncertainty to this, and you need some very powerful processing power to have any reasonable projection. All we can do is rely on data from the past, but unfortunately, we don't live as our parents, and they didn't live the same lifestyle as their parents, so projections for the far distant future are bound to be inaccurate. We also require better and longer medical attention, which means higher bills exactly at the time where we stop earning income. All these factors combined meant a completely new challenge for pension plans they simply hadn't accounted for when traditional plans were at their prime twenty to thirty years ago.

There are even more subtle reasons why most traditional pensions fail. Such plans guaranteed workers a percentage of their salaries for life when they retired, and the burden of that guarantee was on their employer's shoulders. Unfortunately, since the dawn of time, all these pension plans had been calculated with expected returns of 8 percent or more a year, which is, according to John Bogle—founder of Vanguard Group—pure fantasy. He projects that the best they can hope for is 4% a year. This does not include any third-party fees such as administrative expenses or overcharging investment advisors and consultants. The result is that, in any given year, pension plans aren't able to achieve the projected returns, and liabilities pile up.

Passing the Buck

The result of all this has been the rise of the 401(k) plans on both state and corporate level—systems also known as *defined contribution plans* (as opposed the traditional form of *defined benefit plans*). Author Lewis Braham calls January 1st, 1980—the day modern 401(k) plans were introduced—"one of the saddest dates in the history of the American worker." The key reason is that these new plans define only the *contribution*, which is the amount paid *in*, as opposed to promising benefits in the future. This also applies to plans such as 403(b)s, 529s, and individual retirement accounts.

To make matters worse, contributions into these plans aren't mandatory for both employees and employer. Employees who didn't contribute a portion of their own salaries into their plans would not have a safety net. On the other hand, though some companies offer matching contributions up to a set limit, any year a corporation sees itself financially constrained, contributions could be halted. Such plans shifted the burden of a secure retirement onto their members, including passing them the responsibility of figuring out how to structure withdrawals from the savings pot after retirement.

As a result, since the birth of defined contribution plans, many have contributed too little to their 401k—or not at all. About 60% of employees contributed to their 401k plans in 2009, but according to the Employee Benefits Research Institute, the median balance in those plans even before the crash of 2008 was only $18,942. By 2009, it was $12,655.[9] In 2017, these numbers don't look any better.

Retirement and financial experts agree on one point: Americans and workers around the world relying on defined contribution plans will *have* to support themselves through additional, private retirement plans.[10]

How is this new system supposed to work for individuals, when it hasn't worked for giant pension funds with trained personnel and proper resources? The fact of the matter is—no one knows. We know so little about how a market full of little accounts, as opposed to a few big ones, works. Birdthistle called the proliferation of individual retirement accounts a grand experiment:

"—perhaps the richest and riskiest in our financial history—to change the way we save money...The hypothesis of our experiment is that millions of ordinary, untrained, and busy citizens can successfully manage trillions of dollars in a financial system dominated by wealthy, skilled, and powerful investment firms—firms that on many occasions have treated investors shabbily."[11]

John Bogle warns that as a result the US retirement system is "headed for a train wreck."[12] He argues that "when you look at IRA and 401(k), and particularly 401(k) thrift plans—they are thrift plans. They are not retirement plans. They were never designed to be retirement plans, but we're using them to build a retirement plan now, and it simply is not going to work."

Not everyone thinks this is a bad thing. Some would sell us the new reality as libertarian, because we have all the "freedom" to decide our own financial destiny, which is effectively saying "you now have the freedom to be poor." They also—and this is no coincidence—advise us to pass on this newfound freedom to professional money managers and advisors with a direct line to Wall Street. So does this new-found freedom work? As it turns out, not so well.

Recommended Reading:

- Birdthistle, William A. *Empire of the Fund: The Way We Save Now* (Oxford: Oxford University Press, 2016).
- Braham, Lewis. *The House that Bogle Built: How John Bogle and Vanguard Reinvented the Mutual Fund Industry* (New York: McGraw-Hill Education, 2011).
- Butler, Kim D.H. *Busting the Retirement Lies: Living with Passion, Purpose, and Abundance Throughout Our Lives* (Prosperity Economics Movement: 2014)

CHAPTER 2
FAILURE OF THE INDIVIDUALS

Now you are in charge of your own retirement planning and with it the matter of saving and investing for retirement. Listening to financial experts today and you could get the impression that investing for retirement is a child's play. One of the leading financial writers on this subject, William Bernstein (who, coincidentally, also manages money), sums up the conventional path to investing for retirement thus:

> "Start by saving 15 percent of your salary at age 25 into a 401(k) plan, an IRA, or a taxable account (or all three). Put equal amounts of that 15 percent into just three different mutual funds: A U.S. total stock market index fund, an international total stock market index fund, a U.S. total bond market index fund."[13]

Voilà! Your retirement is secured.

With this advice comes a flood of tables and data to substantiate his arguments. They illustrate the power of compounding, the magic of money creating money, and show that stock markets always rise (at least in the US). At the core of all this information is the objective of giving you a motivational boost *to stay the course* for the next 30 to 40 years of diligently working, saving—and, of course, buying more investment funds.

Yet, as Bernstein himself notes, there are a lot of 'ifs' and hurdles to overcome to reap the rewards. The returns will be fabulous *if* the market does go up in a similar fashion to the last 100 years, and *if* you can save 15% of your income for retirement consistently, 30 to 40 years in a row. *If* all the conditions are met, all will be fine, and you will have a stash of money waiting for you. If not, it's your own bloody fault.

Even though there are fierce arguments among financial professionals about the exact ratios and the exact asset mix to rely on, they basically all argue in favor of including a multitude of investment funds in various ratios and combinations. Pretty much all personal finance gurus tow the same line—what I will call the 'conventional wisdom' on retirement planning and investing.[ii] Tony Robbins has the perfect little anecdote to illustrate how investing for retirement is *supposed* to work:

> "I have a self-employed friend who set up her own tax-advantaged retirement account with Vanguard, and she's instructed it to automatically deduct $1,000 from her bank account every month to distribute among her diversified index funds. She knows she might not always have the discipline to buy when one market feels too high or another drops too low, so she takes herself out of the picture. She's a long-term investor who doesn't worry about timing anymore, because her system is automated, and the decision is out of her hands."[14]

Even better for Robbins, she'll probably hire his financial advisory company, which will recommend more of the same for a fee, of

---

[ii] Buy one index funds and stay the course. Bogle; Mr. Money Moustache buy one US stock index fund and one International Stock fund. Buy index funds regularly - Warren Buffett

course (which Robbins' critics estimate to be around 1.5% p.a., and charged in advance each year).[15]

If you want to simplify it even further, follow the advice of John Bogle: Buy one index fund (e.g. Vanguard's VTSAX = Vanguard Total Stock Market Index Fund Admiral Shares) and *stay the course.*

Hence investment funds—or more precisely "mutual funds"— play a central role in how we, the average individual, are supposed to secure our financial future today.

All this begs the question: if it's all as easy as investing in a diversified portfolio, and just sitting back, why are pensions failing and passing on their responsibility to us? And are we—average folk with entire lives to worry about in *addition* to planning for retirement—actually capable of taking on such responsibility, even if it is done through mutual funds? And more importantly, is the standard advice actually working? To answer this, we need to delve deeper into how people tend to behave when it comes to investing for retirement. Be warned; the data isn't pretty.

We Just Can't Save Enough

As iconic thought leader Tim Ferriss summed it up in his best seller *The Four Hour Work Week*:

"Retirement as a goal or final redemption is flawed for at least three solid reasons:

a) It is predicated on the assumption that you dislike what you are doing during the most physically capable years of your life.

b) Most people will never be able to retire and maintain even a hotdogs-for-dinner standard of living.

c) If the math does work, it means that you are one ambitious, hardworking machine."[16]

Point *a* is debatable, but he is spot on with points *b* and *c*. According to an Ernst and Young study, 75% of Americans can expect to see their assets disappear *entirely* before they die. The Center for Retirement Research at Boston College reports that for those workers between the ages of fifty-five and sixty-four, the median balance in household 401(k) or IRA accounts is a scant $111,000. Today, the average American retires at sixty-one and dies at seventy-nine.[17] At our current rates of interest, inflation, and life expectancy, $111,000 would provide only about $7,300 *in each year of a two-decade retirement.* Worse, one-fifth of the workers in this survey hold balances of *less than $13,000 (before* inflation).

The experts have a simple explanation—we just don't save enough, which is a bit like saying somebody is a losing at tennis because he or she is not hitting the ball well enough. Today, most millennials are criticized for leading allegedly hedonistic and wasteful lives. In contrast, many of our parents and grandparents are depicted as leading a solid middle-income life, based on earnest work and delayed gratification so that their retirement could be spent in peace and happiness.

What is perplexing to me is that the criticism usually comes from a generation that works in upper or higher management positions for many companies whose very products and services we are being chided for over-consuming. The companies these people run—as we shall see, the very companies we're supposed to be investing in—succeed on the back of their young consumers' purchases. If you want more head-scratching, just read the business section on how the general economy fares. You will read constant complaints by politician and economists about how sluggish the economy is because we are not consuming enough. The US GDP is roughly 70% personal consumption, and Japan's GDP (the world's third-largest economy) is made up of 60% personal consumption. If we stop buying in order to invest, our investments will shrink as the company's sales decrease. If we do the opposite, we have no savings to grow. *So what exactly are we supposed to do?*

Beyond that, the idea that undergirds standard retirement plans —"linear" earnings growth and spending—is based on the idea that you can put away a little bit from each pay packet every year, and that your pay packet will increase as time goes on. It also assumes that your spending will increase in keeping with your income. But in the real world, nothing is really linear. We tend to spend more in the earlier decades of our lives with peak spending around the age of 50. Houses, children, demanding social lives, and the drive and inclination to explore the world and indulge our interests increase our spending.

Unfortunately, the natural income curve of an average salaried employee doesn't reflect the natural spending pattern. It's much more likely that in those high spending years, we accumulate *debt*, rather than building up a cushy retirement fund. A more natural pattern would be to have higher savings rates later in your career when you can—provided, that you still have a well-paying job, or you are still capable of working three at the same time.

But let's assume you get a job and you are willing to save, it still doesn't add up. If you work about 40 years of your life with an average salary (not everyone can be an investment banker, money manager or business consultant) in order to have enough money saved up to continue living for another 20 years or more, a very high savings rate would be necessary to keep up any remote chance of keeping the same standard of living. But according to the Bureau of Economic Analysis[18], the personal saving rate in the United States is on average 5.7% in 2016—and that is already an improvement to prior years.

And what about those unfortunates—the vast majority of people—without high-paying jobs or jobs at all? You may think that's not you, but according to Oxford University, "Half of today's jobs will be automated within 10 years."[19]Stephen Hawking, the renowned physicist, believes that "artificial intelligence (AI) and increasing automation is going to decimate middle-class jobs… The internet and the platforms that it makes possible allow very small groups of individuals to make enormous profits while employing very few people. This is inevitable, it is progress, but it is also socially destructive."[20]

Whatever the truth behind these forecasts may be, we can assume with confidence that the future will look very different from the lives our parents or grandparents led. All this means is that many of the assumptions at the core of contemporary savings advice simply do not tally with the reality most people face. The result is that in the end, most people simply *cannot* save enough.

But there are other problems too, facing even those who *do* acquire enough money to save—and that is that behaviorally, most people just don't know how to play the market.

We're Not Savvy Investors

Most investors following the conventional approach to retirement investing fall into one of two categories. Either they will blindly follow all the advice given to them, not engaging with their investments in any meaningful way, and end up losing a large chunk of money during a bust cycle—at which point they panic, and, under pressure, withdraw from the market. These people I call *sheep*. The second group reckons they can outwit the market, but don't have a specific edge. When pitted against the smartest Wall Street has to offer, they inevitably come up short. These I call *chipmunks*.

THE SHEEP

The group of sheep is by far the larger group. They are sheep because they blindly follow the lead of their bankers, advisors and TV gurus. They are bamboozled by a slew of jargon. If you ever consulted your banker on the issue of investing for retirement, you might understand what I am talking about. I have seen the process firsthand—I was sitting on the other side of the table wearing a fancy suit, with an expensive pen, and equipped with shiny sales documents featuring lots of graphs and tables. Back in 1999, I was recommending our in-house mutual funds and those funds from investment companies that my bank had a distribution agreement with. Of course, we bankers received a generous distribution fee as a sales incentive. Tech and internet funds were all the rage, and business was good!

Even when people have the resources to sustain losses, the journey can be harrowing and the results disappointing. My own father is a great example. He got lured into the stock market game in 1996 with the introduction of the widely touted Deutsche Telekom AG IPO (Initial Public Offering).[iii] An unprecedented media campaign was launched to promote investing in stocks as the right strategy for the common man and their retirement. And the one stock that would personify this retirement concept would be the stock of Deutsche Telekom AG, which would take care of millions of Germans through stable and secure dividend payments and consistent price increases.

---

iii Deutsche Telekom stock IPO was a complete disaster, when the first internet bubble popped in 2001.

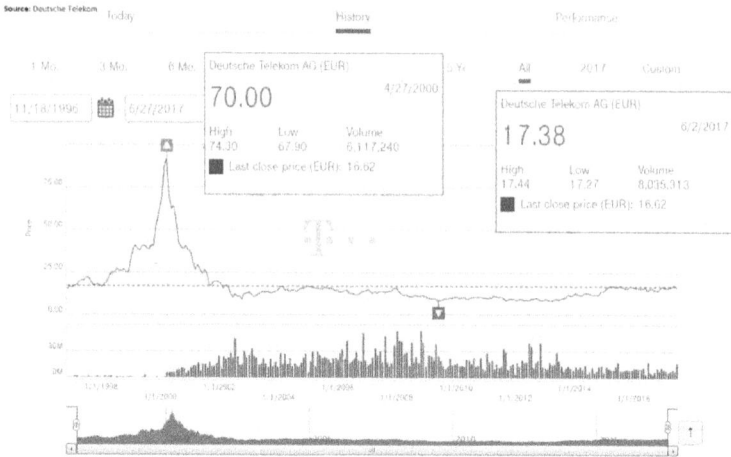

*Source: Deutsche Telekom

In hindsight, it would become a complete disaster, ending with CEO Ron Sommer getting fired, dividend payments cuts, and price volatility that rivaled the Nasdaq's 70% decline in 2001. But the campaign itself was a huge success. It would suck in millions of Germans to a game that lasted right to the end of the tech bubble.

In this first market correction, my father—along with many other Germans—saw his concentrated tech and telecom-weighted portfolio cut by more than half. But unlike other Germans, he followed through with the standard advice you hear from financial advisors when they see their clients panic: to stay the course. Many fellow Germans didn't, and gave up in despair, suffering massive realized losses.

They would soon regret their decision, as an easy monetary policy by Alan Greenspan and other central bankers created a deluge of liquidity that propped up stock markets around the world. Slowly regaining confidence, my father would cautiously buy more stocks at higher prices from 2004 onwards. As markets gained momentum, his initial cautiousness, all of a sudden, turned into open enthusiasm that lasted until 2007.

Unfortunately, he saw his portfolio cut in half again in the carnage of the subprime crisis of 2007/2008. Again, thanks to unprecedented monetary policies (by Ben Bernanke) markets recovered. And so he continues to this day, putting more and more money into stocks, mindful of the next crisis, yet not cashing out while he still can.

Doing a rough calculation on the back of an envelope, his average annualized returns for his entire investment portfolio since 1997 including dividends received, though positive, is disappointing at around 4% p.a. before taxes and not inflation adjusted.

My father is not alone. He is just one of millions of retail investors worldwide, mainly middle-class folks, following conventional advice and the tendency to over-trust their financial advisors and bankers. These clients - conned by the industry and fleeced of their savings - are "sheep." They have no recourse to justice, no sense of how an investment actually works, and they usually end up with scraps, if anything. According to DALBAR, one of the leading industry research firms, "Over a 20-year period, December 31, 1993, through December 31, 2013, the S&P 500 returned an average annual return of 9.28%. However, the average mutual fund investor made just over 2.54%." [21]

The main issues are that they are being charged horrendous fees for very little value, and the timing of buying and selling has been abysmal. In fact, the statistics prove that clients tend to buy into high-risk assets such as equity funds as they are rising, and then, in market corrections, sell at very inopportune moments. Then, they would pull their money out and wait until markets go up again, before re-entering—the very opposite of the cardinal rule of investing: "Buy low, sell high." As Charles Ellis, author of *The Loser's Game*, observed, "The sad result is that investors time and again buy after a fund's best results have been recorded and sell out after the worst performance is over."[22]

The conventional wisdom states that you should just invest at all times, contribute regularly, and above all, *do not panic*.[23] It seems that the vast majority is ignoring this advice, or are simply not capable of following through. You could compare this to the simple advice to eat less and exercise more in order to lose weight. Most of us just can't do it, and it's not always our fault.

Let's consider a very realistic scenario: An individual investor starts dutifully contributing to a standard benchmark index fund of a reputable firm on a monthly basis—this is already considered the pinnacle of sophistication for retail investors, as index funds are low cost and relatively easy to understand. True to theory and expectations, the price of her funds rises, and all is good. Then, disaster strikes. Stock markets drop. A full selling panic breaks out, and prices drop below her average purchase price. For the first time, she is presented with zero gains for all those years of saving. As panic is as infectious as the common cold during winter, she stops contributing to her savings plan (which could lower her average purchase price considerably), but worse, she is forced to sell out of financial need before she loses *everything*. And so ends her foray into financial markets for retirement investing. Staying the course did not help one bit.

What is even more unsettling is the sheer unawareness of clients and their blissful ignorance of fees being charged or adverse performance scenarios. If you ever studied the court papers of disgruntled clients who sued mutual funds companies such as BlackRock or Fidelity, you will see a clear pattern emerge.

- Clients regularly underestimate the real fees involved even for index fund investments.
- Clients are confused by the product variety of today's mutual fund and ETF universe.
- Clients have unreasonable return expectations induced by over-optimistic advertising.

And that is the sad truth of how most sheep experience the stock market—they lose, they get bamboozled, and there's not a damn thing they can do about it.

THE CHIPMUNKS

The more impatient among us—chipmunks—want to speed things up. They embrace the freedom they've gained by taking possession of their own retirement funds, and are dissatisfied with historical returns of 8 to 9% p.a. They read up on theory and strategies, and convince themselves that with their superior drive and knowledge, they can beat the markets by a wide margin and earn a decent living by trading every day. In reality, like real chipmunks (who can live up to nine years in captivity, but are usually gobbled up by something within three years in the wild), the odds of winning are consistently stacked against them from the start. Sure, there are winners, but the percentage of *consistent* winners is negligible. The bleak reality is that the longer those few successful players stay in the game, the higher the chances are that they will experience a massive blow to their bankrolls.

A great example of speculator's paradox is the infamous Jesse L. Livermore. Edwin Lefèvre's biography, *Reminiscences of a Stock Operator*, describes how this early investment pioneer won, and lost, and won again—before finally losing it all, and killing himself over his failure. Adolf Merckle, a German with a net worth of $12 billion from a pharmaceutical business empire he controlled like a good old-fashioned patriarch, also committed suicide after he lost billions in a highly speculative trade involving Volkswagen and Porsche in 2009. According to family and friends, his behavior was a "complex combination of pride, guilt over what he saw as failing his family, and, perhaps most importantly, loss of control."[24]

Many traders and gamblers play the markets for more mundane reasons. If you visit any stock market or trading floor of any kind, you will hear fascinating stories of how many of these professional traders and speculators made fortunes trading for their own accounts, only to lose it in one or two bad trades. Ironically, what has always kept them afloat and away from the poorhouse has been their jobs on the trading floors: to sell bets to the even less fortunate—the sheep. Wall Street attracts "suckers" like the sirens did the Greek sailors in the *Odyssey*.

My Own Odyssey

I, too, had dreams of quick and easy riches with the help of Wall Street. I was introduced to the world of stock markets in early 1994 through my local bank, Stadtsparkasse Moenchengladbach. They sponsored a game that introduced high school students to the fascinating world of stock markets. It was supposed to teach us about the importance of investing for retirement (how many 16-year-olds do you know that are saving for their retirement?) What it really provided was a pile of Gordon Gekko-type propaganda about the glory of chasing hot stock tips and wild speculations on currencies and anything that moved widely and you could bet money on. Instead of becoming responsible investors for retirement, we became de facto gamblers.

But the game didn't end there, at least not for me. I wanted more, and I wanted to work for the investment banking world, a dream that would lead from the trading floors of sleepy Dusseldorf to London, Tokyo, and Singapore. I studied everything that I was supposed to study when playing the game, except the actual topic of investing, and ended up trading like a madman. I became a full-blown speculator, increasingly using more and more financial leverage, growing overconfident in my trading. The results were as unsurprising as they were devastating. Thankfully, I learned my lessons, because I had to. I realized I never really grasped the importance of understanding businesses that generate cash flows and create value. Instead, I was more interested in speculating on *price differentials* of stocks, mutual funds and currencies markets. To quote Keynes:

"We have reached the third degree where we devote our intelligence to anticipating what average opinion expects the average opinion to be."

It truly was absurd! For example, I speculated on how other currency traders would react before each Federal Reserve meeting or how Microsoft's share prices would react after quarterly earnings announcements, at times even *before* they were announced. All that mattered was to anticipate the next price movement upwards or downwards and place bets accordingly. It detached me from the real principles of investing: understanding businesses and cash flows.

Any statistic collected from brokers and online brokers confirm that a very large percentage lose money day-trading. A common ball-park figure is that 90 to 95% of all traders lose money. Eighty percent of all day traders quit within the first two years, only to return in the next boom period. The average individual investor *underperforms* market indices by 1.5% per year. Active traders underperform by *6.5%* annually. And so...

Most of us are neither made for saving, nor for modern financial markets investing. For those of us who are able to save diligently, the money goes straight to Wall Street. Many fall victim to cognitive biases. As Richard Thaler writes in *Misbehaving: The Making of Behavioral Economics*:

Humans do not have the brains of Einstein (or Barro), nor do they have the self-control of an ascetic Buddhist monk. Rather, they have passions, faulty telescopes, treat various pots of wealth quite differently, and can be influenced by short-run returns in the stock market.[25]

Strangely enough, there seems to be one small group who is relentless in promoting the existing ways without offering alternatives. The group contains an exclusive network of financial interests that has seen explosive growth and enormous financial rewards for themselves. As we shall see, this is all on the back of consumers who had to deal with a new reality; certainly, more than they had ever bargained for. In chapter 3, the final chapter of Part I, we will take a closer look at this group and the inherent flaws and structural shortcomings of the system they represent.

Recommended Reading:

- Mahar, Maggie. *Bull!: A History of the Boom and Bust, 1982-2004* (London: HarperCollins 2009)
- Livermore, Jesse L. *Reminiscences of a Stock Operator* (New York: John Wiley & Sons, 1923)
- Schwager, Jack D. *Market Wizards: Interview with Top Traders.* (HarperCollins, 1989)
- Keynes, John Maynard. *The General Theory of Employment, Interest and Money.* (London: Palgrave MacMillan, 1936)

CHAPTER 3
FAILURE OF THE INDUSTRY

In chapters 1 and 2, we've seen how the pension system is bankrupt, and how the responsibility for a financially secure retirement is now in the hands of individuals who are often overwhelmed and unprepared for the responsibility. We've seen that most of us aren't very good at saving and, furthermore, are ill-equipped to deal with the psychological burden of investing. This is the way the elites who run the investing world like it. A small group is actually profiting from this and work hard to attract even the youngest among us disguised as "financial education" and "retirement planning." I am talking, of course, about Wall Street, and the mutual fund industry.

In this chapter, I will discuss how a few corporations have reached gigantic proportions and how they achieved their growth and profitability. I will list the effects of the system they've created, which is primarily geared towards benefitting them; it saddles their customers with subpar performance, and keeps them largely ignorant about what is going on. I will argue that the result is as tragic as it is illogical—and therefore, so is continuing to buy into traditional investment-for-retirement schemes.

The Idea of Capital Markets

Historically, the king of all assets has been land and property. The only problem is that most of us can't get hold of it. It's either out of reach or simply too expensive, as the demand for good land is always high. After all, land is limited; so those in possession of it, don't give it up easily. The same counts for traditional business ownership. Besides the substantial risks, if you don't know what you are doing, giant corporations dominate their industries, have a global reach and have all the advantages that size and money brings. It's impossible to compete with the giant corporations head on.

Financial markets aimed to solve these challenges by enabling individuals with less financial resources to participate through smaller stakes and passing on the management responsibility to professionals. It would also spread any financial risks from one party to several participants. At the same time, all the money pooled from these participants provided liquidity and precious risk capital for any large-scale projects imaginable. In the 17th and 18th centuries, it was all about financing lucrative new-world explorations and trade. In the 19th century, early financial markets would more and more finance the industrial revolution which turned into a full-blown economic revolution that encompassed the entire globe ranging from technology to medicine and modern warfare. In short, it powered growth (and growth demands more and more capital, and more and more participants). As useful and important as this new system was for financing growth and progress, it came with some serious side effects.

Financial markets are trading place for buying and selling of existing ownership rights in large economic endeavors known as securities. It's a place where you can purchase or trade other people's income producing assets, issues in units of securities, which range from business ownerships, land and property ownerships to all sorts of debt certificates, such as Treasury or corporate bonds of different maturities. And its core function is to set prices for all those assets traded.

If you bought someone else's asset in a private transaction, you would negotiate your purchase or selling price. It has always been an inefficient and lengthy process riddled with traps for both sides. Today's financial markets aim to offer a convenient place to circumvent all these challenges, but it literally comes at a price and the risk of complacency.

For example, if someone doesn't tell you that the house you want to purchase has a serious plumbing issue, you most certainly would overpay underestimating the additional repairs necessary. However, you would make sure that would never happen. It is called due diligence or simply doing your homework before you pay the price. As a buyer, it would be your own responsibility to make sure you don't buy a lemon—buyer beware—caveat emptor. In financial markets, most buyers of securities wouldn't even be aware that there is a plumbing system, let alone the possibility of a plumbing issue of sorts. All that counts is the popularity of a specific security or even mutual funds and its potential to rise in price in the foreseeable future. How that might work out and on what grounds is left to the experts to explain. They will always come up with all sorts of clever sounding justifications and explanations, because it's their job and they are good at it. To quote Buffett: "Never ask a barber if you need a haircut!"

As previously discussed, market prices seem to have magic power over us. Financial markets seem the only place where popularity trumps rational cash flow considerations. The greater fool theory comes to mind:

> "The price of an object is determined not by its intrinsic value, but rather by irrational beliefs and expectations of market participants. A price can be justified by a rational buyer under the belief that another party is willing to pay an even higher price."[26]

If you pay prices purely based on popularity, you are bound to get disappointed, because popularity is in the eye of the beholder and it always changes—it's called fads. But, the reverse is also true. Remember, nothing is more infectious than fear and panic. Stampede is truly a great word to describe the occasional market crashes, panics, and sheer insanity among financial market investors. It truly is irrational, and even those that could ignore the folly are captured and drawn into the *madness of crowds*.

Sucked into Index Investing

Investment returns either come in the form of regular income in accordance or through sporadically buying and selling assets, also known as capital gains. Both types of cash flows combined are called *total returns*. For example, if you own rental property, you receive monthly rental income. If you sell your property at a higher price than you purchased it, you will receive additional income from price increases. Interest income from savings or fixed income securities and capital gains from buying and selling stocks and mutual funds are today's standard form of cash flows. Unfortunately, over the last three decades, more and more capital gains have been overemphasized for some very obvious reasons, but the consequences for all can be severe.

Today, we have a new reality with general interest rates at near zero. Similar to professional pension funds, many retail investors feel they have no other choice than to chase higher yielding risk assets to compensate for the lack of interest income and inability to save more of their monthly paychecks. And similar to the GPIF, they neither have the capability nor motivation to deal with the complexity of a system that seems alien to them. But unlike GPIF and other pension funds, they don't have the resources nor training to keep a close eye on their portfolios and on those that advice and manage them. Hence, they become the sheep in the big money game.

Today, through the rise of individual retirement accounts, this number has swelled to more than $15 trillion, with $6.9 trillion kept in 401(k)s—most of that in equity funds.[27] But it was not always this way. Investing in mutual funds didn't become mainstream until the early 1980s. At the start of 1982, only $241 billion was managed by mutual funds. In fact, investing in stocks wasn't a mainstream tendency until the 1990s. At the start of 1982, only $41 billion of the $241 billion managed by fund managers was in equity; the remainder was in bonds ($14 billion) and by far the largest part was placed into conservative money market funds ($186 billion). At the end of 1990, assets in bond ($291 billion) and money market ($498 billion) funds still outnumbered assets in stock funds($239 billion) three to one.[28]

During that period, there simply wasn't a need for higher-risk investment vehicles. The preferred choice of retirement savings, besides corporate pensions and social security contributions, were fixed income deposits, real estate, and a combination of gold and other valuables collected over decades. I remember when my mother would regularly visit her local bank to roll over our fixed-term deposits and commercial paper investments, both of which paid interest every 3 or 6 months. They were transparent, and there was no need to study financial markets. She knew she would get her money back after each term, and a healthy portion of interest on top of that. She could tell exactly what each bank would charge her in fees, and how much she owed to the taxman.

But with the meteoric rise of mutual funds in the United States through the introduction of defined benefit plans (401k), things changed dramatically. By the end of 1996, equity funds exceeded other asset classes for the first time. Today, equity mutual funds dominate individual retirements accounts with either actively managed mutual funds or equity index funds and ETFs.

The institutions that barged into the pension market have a long history of capitalizing on people's investment dreams. Just take a look at the explosive growth of some of these entities. Fidelity traces its beginnings back to 1946 when founder Edward C. Johnson II managed a few million for his clients. Today, the Fidelity Group commands a $6 trillion empire, a mind boggling growth, even adjusting for inflation. Meanwhile, the Vanguard group, established in 1975, started with just $11 million for its first index fund. As of early 2017, they manage over $4 trillion. The compensation package for managers in these firms easily reaches the tens of millions of dollars per year. Larry Fink, co-founder and CEO of BlackRock, the largest asset manager in the world with

$5.4 trillion AUM, was awarded $25.8 million in compensation in 2015, compared with $23.9 million in 2014.[29]

These Wall Street firms live off market share. Their mission is simple—growth at any cost. In the case of retirement investment, your savings are the fuel that powers it. We can see the same in the field of index funds and ETFs. Providers offer both low-cost index funds and traditional mutual funds with much higher fee structures. Clients are drawn in with lower fee products, but are then incentivized to buying higher fee products. That this business model works can be seen by the constant growth of market share they are taking away from traditional mutual fund providers. The whole index fund world has ballooned to over 30% of all mutual fund assets in 2016 with strong momentum going forward. Within this 30%, Black Rock is already the largest asset manager in the world; Vanguard, the largest mutual fund provider in the world; and State Street is the owner of the largest ETF in the world.

Problem 1: They Suck You Dry

Today, mutual funds are the central investment tool for the retail masses around the world. This is how we all are supposed to save and invest for retirement. If you enter any local bank or visit a financial advisor in an industrialized country, they will have a wide range of mutual funds on offer. If you read any standard financial literature, including those produced by famed personal finance gurus, mutual funds will be on the top of their recommendation list supplemented with life-insurance products.

But, mutual funds are no panacea. There are no standard instructions on how to use them and how to structure them in a way that suits your financial situation or payout requirements at the time of retirement. Pension programs, on the other hand, would be in charge of tasks ranging from administering your accounts to making sure that you get paid after you entered your retirement period. Like in the case of the GPIF, you would never be bothered about how to correctly and prudently structure your asset portion.

A team of professional pension managers and administrators watch over that function, and the tasks they can't do themselves are outsourced to third parties- but, with a big difference. There is accountability to one central and powerful pension board.

On the contrary, in an individual retirement account, such as a 401k, all these tasks have to be done by the contributing member. Not to mention the higher fees involved when managing millions of individual accounts separately. For example, mutual fund managers act, under no duty, to generate streams of payments to people who are no longer working. The task of choosing the right mutual funds among thousands (8000 funds in the US alone)—in the right proportions in accordance with future cash flow requirements and changing risk tolerance—falls to each client. Overexposure to equities could have fatal consequences if stock markets crashed just before your retirement. There might not be enough time left for a substantial recovery before you would be forced to sell in order to satisfy your yearly cash requirements. An index fund would never warn you about such things; that's not its function.

Furthermore, the constant portfolio rebalancing, assessment of financial risks and management of cash flow requirements represent a daunting task to the average individual. Some would naturally consult financial advisors, and opt to pay for services pension funds would provide free of charge. But where pension funds manage their responsibilities efficiently and centrally, individuals have to cope not only with higher fees for each financial product they purchase, and the additional fees charged by the plan provider that's administering their 401(k) plan, but also the fees paid for financial advice and customization of portfolios.

In a worst case scenario, a typical retail investor could end up paying 2 to 3% to generic mutual funds, plus 401(k) administrative fees, and a fixed annual fee of 1% or more for financial advice. It's a fee bonanza but not for you, the individual investor. This model could work, if the market consistently yielded 8 to 9% as they did in the past. In a new market reality with 5% or even fewer return expectations, those fees can quickly eat up most of the investment returns. Unlike traditional pension funds that promised stable streams of income through defined benefit plans, neither mutual funds nor financial advisors promise any performance results or give guarantees for future cash payouts.

In *MONEY: Master the Game,* Tony Robbins vehemently argues that mutual funds and 401(k) administrators are cheating clients on expense ratios, and hence their retirement future. According to Robbins, traditional mutual funds charge much higher fees than clients usually assume. For example, clients would buy mutual funds in the expectation that they would pay around 1 to 1.5% for buying a standard mutual fund, but they were later presented with a bill that ballooned to 3% or even 4% of what they have invested in those funds. Also, clients often underestimated the hidden deductions within the fund itself. Payment to brokers, IT vendors and research service providers quickly add up. When clients want out, they were presented with another set of fees ranging from penalty fees to simple closing fees.30

As an example, a difference between paying 0.25% to 1% might be the small amount of just 0.75%, but the cumulative effects over time are enormous. Higher fees mean less money for you to invest, hence less future returns. If the difference in fees is compounded over 20 to 30 years, the lost gains are enormous. Projections indicate that with a 0.75% fee difference, with an average US salary, you could have *$70,000* less by the time you retire at age 65.[31] The difference could mean three years of additional work to make up the savings gap. You can imagine what the impact would be if your real fees are 3% per year, instead of the 0.25% or 1%.[iv] As John Bogle said, "The more the managers and brokers take, the less the investors make." The ironic thing is index fund providers, including Vanguard, are in the business of collecting fees.

[iv] Assuming a median salary of $30,500 between the ages of 25 to 34 after which their income increases in accordance with past compensation date

However, they do it from a much lower cost basis and with a different business model to increase their sales and profitability.

Problem 2: Corruption

Besides hidden fees and opposing financial interests, the mutual fund industry has always been riddled with structural and regulatory flaws that have been outright harmful to their clients. Their list of transgressions ranges from front-running clients and late trading, to simple insider trading on both sides of the trade.

The textbook definition of "front running" is "the practice by market-makers of dealing on advance information provided by their brokers and investment analysts, before their clients have been given the information." It simply means that a party with fiduciary duties is in possession of order information about their client's immediate investment decisions. Hence, they can overcharge their own clients or sell this information to a third party for a cut of the trading profits. Wall Street and the mutual fund industry have taken front running to a whole new level. In 2003, New York Attorney General Eliot Spitzer began to investigate a spate of illegal late trades and suspicious market activities involving some leading mutual fund providers and hedge funds. After an investigation, it became apparent that some hedge and mutual funds were cooperating with each other to maximize their profits through illegal late trading in mutual fund pricing. It basically meant that a few hedge funds were allowed to travel back in time, by buying mutual funds at prior closing prices knowing that prices would rise in early morning trading. Easy and quick profits on the back of less well-connected investors.

The depth and reach of the scandal in 2003, which involved names such as Putnam Investments, Janus, and Invesco, shocked even the most hardened clients. The Securities & Exchange Commission (SEC) launched its own investigation in 2003, which uncovered even more dubious practices among the leading mutual fund companies. It included insider trading by participants on both sides of the trade, by fund managers and their brokers, and traditional front running in individual stock holdings. The SEC claimed that "certain mutual fund companies alerted favored customers or partners when one or more of a company's funds planned to buy or sell a large stock position. The partner was then in a position to trade shares of the stock in advance of the fund's trading. Since mutual funds tend to hold large positions in specific stocks, any large sales or purchases by the fund often impact the value of the stock, from which the partner could stand to benefit."

All these scandals came to light in the aftermath of the Dotcom bubble burst and the economic consequences of 9/11. The second wave of scandals involving mutual funds and money managers came in the aftermath of the subprime crisis—ranging from stuffing mutual funds with risky securities that shouldn't have been in there, to the dramatically-named "Target Date Funds Massacres."

Target Date funds are mutual funds that take over the asset allocation task for their clients in order to have liquidity at the time of their retirement. They are an ideal investment vehicle for those passive investors who don't want to deal with managing the ratios between asset classes such as bonds, cash, and equities. Instead, the fund managers at Target Date funds balances the asset ratios for their fund holders in accordance with liquidity requirements that revolves a specific target date. As the name suggests, these funds are structured around a fixed target date that represents the start of the withdrawal phase. Hence, funds with target dates of around 2010 were supposed to be almost risk-free with liquid cash and bond holdings rather than risky stock positions. The reality looked very different. Their holders suffered losses as high as 40% like any general stock market mutual fund during the subprime crisis, even though they were supposed to be conservative as the target date were just two years later. You can imagine how the fund holders felt when they were presented with the bill at a time when they were preparing for a life of traveling or pursuing their life dreams.

We can only guess what the next wave of scandals will hold for us when we experience another financial crisis. Just remember, information is everything in this business, and those who have it can be tempted to misappropriate such information. Giant money management firms and brokers sit at the very epicenter of valuable information. Where there is a high concentration of money, an excessive incentive system in place, and powerful interests competing for market dominance, there are always irregularities. In the meantime, we are encouraged to participate, and more importantly, to contribute to the very same system that powers their growth.

Problem 3: Lousy Returns

All of these flaws and irregularities on fund level—combined with the inadequacy and incompetence by the individual retail investors—is terrible news for returns. To refresh your memory, where the normal market index would have scored around 9.28% annual returns in the in a 20 year period from December 1993 to December 2013, the average mutual fund investor made just over 2.54%. This period included one of the most prosperous periods and bull markets in global stock history, as is coincided with the rise of the Internet and advancing globalization.

One reason for this, as Warren Buffett himself explains, is that financial markets move in "megacycles." In one of his rare contributions to *Fortune*, he points out that in the 17 years from December, 1964 to December, 1981, the Dow Jones Industrial Index began at 874.12 and ended at 875—a rise of precisely zilch. He stresses that during that same 17 years, "the GDP of the U.S. —that is, the business being done in this country—almost quintupled, rising by 370%." On the other hand, the following 17 years, from 1981 to 1998, were just phenomenal for stock markets in the US. Starting from 875.00 in December 1981, the Dow Jones would trade at 9181.43 in December 1998, a phenomenal 1000% increase. And yet, the economy would only grow by 177% for the same period. So, if it is not the economy that actually determines the size of the stock market, what does? Well, to grossly oversimplify his conclusion, Buffett believes the main determinant of these opposing performance periods has something to do with changing interest environments. The first period experienced peak Fed benchmark rates of up to 13% in July 1974, whereas the second period saw interest rates decline to almost zero, stimulating growth, money lending, and all that capitalistic jazz.

Today, interests seem ready to creep up again—where else could they go from an almost zero, if not upwards? As of writing in June 2017, The Fed benchmark was set at 1.25%, already an increase of 100 basis point from an all-time low of 0.25% in December 2008.

Furthermore, the profitability projections by major companies seem to be on a downward trend with many CEOs openly cautious—among them, Bernard Arnaud the CEO of LVMH, the world's biggest luxury group. He was quoted as saying, "My sentiment for 2017 is one of caution," and, "The economic climate, the present situation is... scary."[32]

Worldwide investors and the companies they invest in find it (on average) very difficult to make high single digit returns on their capital, let alone double digit returns (unless they leverage themselves up to the hilt). Not to go into too much detail, but the cause is a unique combination of the enormous size of the leading stock companies these days, increased global competition, general slower economic growth, and very low-interest rates and easy money. The combination of all these factors means lower expected returns for shareholders. If you don't believe me, here are return forecasts from the man who should know about market returns-John Bogle, himself:

> "Just for mathematical reasons, the dividend yield is 2 percent, a little under 2 percent in fact, and the long-term dividend yield on stocks is pretty close to 4 ... the

earnings growth on stocks has been a little over 5, that's going to be a very tough target in the future so let's call it 4 ... 4 and 2 percent give you a 6 percent investment return, but then you have to take ... the valuations in the market. ...You take that 6 percent return and maybe knock it off a couple of points perhaps for a lower valuation, slightly lower valuation over a decade and you're talking about a 4 percent nominal return on stocks. And that's low, lower than history. History is around 6 and a half."[33]

Over the last two decades, he has already adjusted his stock market return forecasts downwards from the standard 9% down to 7%, and to 4% in March 2017.

Bogle is the strongest proponent of what is known as a 'dumbed down' asset allocation strategy, arguing that "when you understand how our financial markets actually work, you will see that the index fund is indeed the only investment that guarantees you will capture your fair share."[34] But, what if fair market returns are disappointingly low and the risk enormous? He confirms that the risks are "quite large" when you put your money into equities. So, maybe not the best idea.

Let's give it the benefit of the doubt, and assume for a moment the majority of investors with a standard equity-heavy allocation do make 5% per year. Now I ask you, if I were to give you a wager that could make you 5% if you win, but could cost you 50% - would you take that bet? Certainly not, but don't deceive yourself, that is what investing in mutual funds means these days.

Problem 4: Bubbles and Irrationality

Another disturbing reality of retirement investing today is that nothing is more important to stock and mutual fund returns than market prices. The reason is simple: the main determinant of your performance is the average purchase price of all your past purchases. If the average price of all your purchases is lower than the current market price, you can account for a book gain. The reverse is also true: if the price moves lower than your average purchase price, you will need to account for a book loss. Regular income has no or very little meaning. Remember: it's all about growth. This system contains a whole lot of potential for mischief.

Firstly, an over-fixation on prices encourages speculation that could lead to outright gambling. As a matter of fact, the whole premise of modern retirement investing is based on a big gamble-the hope of higher prices in the future.

But what are the consequences if the reverse happens? Will you be able to sell at a high price at exactly the moment you start cashing out? Even diehard believers get nervous when they see their portfolios down by 30% or more for several months in a row. What happens if months turn to years and stock markets don't recover? If that seems unlikely, take a look at the Japanese stock market. The Nikkei still trades below its peak from 1989 of 38,700. As of June 2017, nearly a 27 years after it crashed, it hovers at 20,000.

Financial markets operate on a simple demand and supply principle. They are gauges for any fad and folly imaginable, and often have no basis in rationality—as Tulip Mania, the South Sea Bubble, and the Dotcom crash all showed. Today, our retirement planning is entirely based on a system with devastating consequences for the future. As we have seen from the beginning, individuals are now tasked with balancing the proper ratios of various asset classes in their personal portfolios themselves. They need to rebalance between cash and non-price sensitive assets but low yielding, to high-risk asset classes that rely on capital gains but are volatile in nature. Not an easy task if you understand human nature.

A team of behavioral economists showed that when investors in retirement plans earn high returns, making them richer, they increase their saving rates that go straight into stock markets, most likely because they extrapolate this investment success into the future. This behavioral pattern has not changed, and even in 2017, we see this same pattern in full swing.

Problem 5: You Learn Zero

Today, we have a myriad of retirement calculators that can calculate the exact amount of money you need to save today, so that you can retire with the same standard of living tomorrow. At the same time, they will spit out a customized pie charts with exact instructions of how it should be implemented through mutual funds. You just have to tweak some numbers, add some higher yielding asset here, allocate some money there, and ready is your pizza pie with 8 slices or more. All this should assure you that retirement planning is as easy as tuning your radio and as mechanical as calculating the position of stars and planets. All this is to encourage you to continue contributing and to remain invested on Wall Street's terms. In the end, you get away with a false sense of security, and a system that entirely relies on the fate of future market prices.

In this perfect world of predictable returns and constant growth, you are encouraged to ignore all boom and bust cycles and the constant skullduggery on Wall Street. You will be assured that these have no meaning in the long-term. They will be like *blips* on a wonderful chart that always points upwards.

The message is clear: ignore everything and look forward. Ignore the ridiculous financial excesses of the past. Shuffle the money on a monthly basis, in a multitude of financial product offerings. Don't get involved and don't ask questions. Ignore all the filth and rotten practices that seem to come to light with each economic bust.

It all comes to this: it's OK to know nothing. If you believe the above, then I am afraid to say, you are being conned. You are being lulled into a false sense of security where in any future financial crisis, you will neither have learned the mechanics of investing nor be prepared for the logical consequences. Job losses are real consequences, and being forced to sell your stocks, mutual funds, and ETFs, at the worst possible moment, are some of the psychological traumas you might have to deal with in a time of sheer panic. You won't even know whom to blame for your miserable financial situation. Try to sue any of the mutual fund providers, and you'll discover it's pretty much impossible. In the end, you haven't learned anything of value, except how to transfer money from your pockets to someone else's. You have always been, and remain, a "know-nothing" member to the party.

Part I Summary

As Thomas Friedman observes, "It is a 401(k) world;" "Government will do less for you. Companies will do less for you."[35] In short, employers, both private and public, will continue shifting the costs and risks of future payouts to employees. The key reasons are the unpredictability of returns and uncertain financial obligations.

What all experts agree on is that the current system is heading for a train wreck. But instead of coming up with valid alternatives, they offer the same medicine in slightly different dosages. We are encouraged to follow in pension funds' footsteps by doing pretty much the same thing they do, but on our own watch, and at a much higher cost.

Ask yourself: If following their generic investment advice and retirement platitudes are as easy and as simple as we're told, why are neither governments nor private employers willing to bear the responsibility of managing our pension plans? They used to manage pension plans, and they have the power and capability to deduct the exact amounts from our paychecks and pool the money into a giant, professionally managed funds.[v] With the size of their

---

[v] Yes, index funds are also professionally managed mutual funds – you wouldn't want anything less.

pots of money, they could negotiate very competitive fees with any service provider. They could hire professionals whose only mission is to avoid all the "ifs" and "buts." More importantly, these professionals would be accountable to powerful organizations, instead of single individuals who have none of the influence or power to make their rights heard. Do you know what the answer to that is?

As it is written in the Economist: "Whether we like it or not, we are going back to the pre-Bismarckian world, where work had no formal stopping point."[36] The middle class might as well be dead already, as they are squeezed by a different job reality on one end and mismanagement of their little financial resources on the other. What perspective does this give to millennials who follow in the footsteps of a generation that might be called a financial failure in retirement?

The retirement system as it exists today is broken, and with the impending financial crisis that is sure to come, it's not only the end of the middle class, but also the end of retirement as we know it. We are set up for financial failure, and we remain the know-nothing party in the game. The result will be more risk taking and more dependency on the same system for lack of alternatives. It's a vicious cycle.

If you have understood the seriousness of the flaws of our current retirement system the resulting financial risks for your well-being, there is no other alternative than to choose a radically different path. Part II will show you how this path looks like and why you can only benefit from it (you can't lose).

Recommended Reading

- Braham, Lewis: *The House that Bogle Built: How John Bogle and Vanguard Reinvented the Mutual Fund Industry.* (New York: McGraw-Hill Education, 2011)
- Thaler, Richard. *Misbehaving. The Making of Behavioral Economics.* (New York: W. W. Norton & Company. 2016)
- Robbins, Tony. *MONEY Master the Game: 7 Simple Steps to Financial Freedom.* (New York: Simon & Schuster; 2014)

THE DEATH OF RETIREMENT

PART II

ACTIONABLE ADVICE

CHAPTER 4
THE CONVENTIONAL ROUTE

There is a debate among financial experts and economists about why so few of us save wisely and fail to achieve market returns. Some of their conclusions include:

- The system doesn't work mathematically. The savings required are unrealistic for the vast majority of people, due to decaying job security and uncertain stock market returns.
- It's too abstract. Many of us don't want to live our lives for the sake of some mythical halcyon retirement. We want to enjoy life while we can.
- People are neither incentivized to save nor do they get a proper introduction to investing. Many often confuse investing with plain speculation, which, many times, turns into gambling.
- The current system invites fraud and misappropriation on a massive scale, which has undermined confidence and trust in those whom you should be giving your money to.

The list could go on, but you get the point. Bottom line: as *The Economist* has bluntly put it, "Give up any hope of ever retiring." in the way that your parents did.[37]

This might be a bit of downer, but there is a lot of good that can come from it. Humans are extremely resilient, especially in times of adversity. You can be one or two steps ahead of the game, if you embrace this new reality today, and this starts with learning about all available options. What we need is a base education that clarifies the true nature of saving and investing, and that offers a few strategies that are more in sync with how we, as imperfect humans, deal with abstract concepts like delayed gratification, compound interest, and investing for an uncertain future.

The most challenging subject within all this is investing. Here, what is needed is a clear understanding of what investing means and what it could encompass that will ultimately give you an edge over those who try to take advantage of you.

In this chapter, we'll take a look at the conventional options available to you *now*. This means social security, corporate pensions, and private pension plans. We'll also take a look at what you can expect, if you choose to rely on them, and what hurdles you'll have to overcome to do so. Be warned—they are formidable.

Social Security

Social security benefits vary by country. In the US, the Social Security Act was signed into law by Franklin Roosevelt in 1935, and encompasses several social welfare and social insurance programs, disability insurance, and basic pensions. You can claim Social Security at age 62 the earliest, to age 70 the latest. America's social security system is funded primarily through payroll taxes collected by the IRS.

For comparison, the German system, which actually dates back to the 19th century, has three separate sections. The 'State Pension Insurance' applies to all employees and employers paying a percentage of salaries into this system. The other two sections are a 'Voluntary Occupational Pension Insurance' and private insurance. Funds paid in by contributors (employees and employers) are not saved (or invested), but are used to pay current pension obligations.

This poses a serious problem. With one of the worst demographics among industrialized countries, there is less and less money in the pot to support a growing population. The retirement age was increased to 66 recently, and it will be increased again, by 2023, to 67. In 2012, the average pension was a scant €1263.15 ($1,600) per month.

These circumstances are repeated all over the world, including in Japan. What this means for you, provided you've been paying into your state pension, is that payouts might not be enough to cover the bare minimum of your future needs. But, it's a start that many *developing countries* don't provide. Keep in mind that this is just the first layer of retirement defense in US retirement planning and for countries such as Germany or Japan. There are two more layers to follow.

Employer Pension Plans

For most employees in the US and other first-world countries, there will also be access to some form of individual work-based retirement plan either through government, corporate or trade-union controlled options.

The 401(k), has become the dominant retirement savings plan sponsored by an employer in the US and has spread to other developed countries. A good example of such a plan can be seen with the Thrift Savings Plan (TSP), a savings plan the federal government offers to its employees in the US. As a government sponsored thrift plan, it comes with very attractive fee structures. Members only have to pay fees as low as 2.9 basis points, or 0.029 percent of what they contribute—far less than almost every other mutual fund or ETF charges to general retail clients in America. The low fees result from economies of scale and the subsequent bargaining power afforded to the institution by more than 4.6 million participants and more than $400 billion in assets.[38] Its funds are mainly managed by BlackRock, the largest asset manager in the world.

So, here is a small dose of straight talk from financial journalist Felix Salmon:

"The 401(k) is a way for both your government and your employer to disown you, and to leave your life savings to be raided by the financial-services industry and its plethora of hidden and invidious fees."[39]

Neither straight-talking, self-made millionaire Grant Cardone nor I could agree more. Cardone calls 401(k)s, and other retirement savings accounts, "traps that prevent people from ever having enough."[40]

Keep in mind, original pension plans and their successor, the 401k, were designed to be *tax efficient* savings plans for future retirement needs—a form of additional retirement insurance beyond basic social security. They do offer real benefits to many participants who would prefer a very passive approach to their financial affairs. But they are not, as many personal finance gurus suggest, a simple path to wealth.

Private Pension Plans

A private pension is a plan where individuals contribute from their earnings, which then pays a private pension after retirement, in addition to what may be received from Social Security or any corporate 401(k) plan. It's the third defensive layer, and is an alternative for anyone who opts out of state, or corporate schemes, or wouldn't be covered by them in the first place, such as the self-employed, or employees at small to midsize companies. In many cases, contributions to such plans are tax deductible.

One distinct characteristic of most private pension plans is that the holder themselves have to manage their withdrawal rates and account balances. That is one of the main features of any defined contribution plan. By definition, only the contributions are defined not the benefits and all the management that come with it. Investment risks and pension balance risks are not borne by the plan sponsor but by the plan holder—and this is the primary issue of retirement planning for individuals.

In the USA, a very popular vehicle for private pension plans is the Individual Retirement Account (IRA). The IRA has tax benefits, and is easily accessible. The standard IRA is held at a custodian institution, such as a bank or brokerage, that will give you options on how you could store or invest your savings contributions. For example, the custodian may allow plain certificates of deposit, individual stocks and mutual fund holdings.

Another option that falls under private pensions is various forms of life insurance products run by insurance companies. These elaborate contracts will pay out a regular pension at a specific retirement date, depending on the contract's details and agreements. A popular form of insurance is 'Term Life Insurance,' which protects a family if the main breadwinner passes away. Some financial advisors recommend whole life insurance products, policies which remain in force for the insured's entire lifetime, provided required premiums are paid, or to the maturity date.[41]

With all private pension plan solutions, including those offered by your employer, you need to keep one thing in mind: Private pension plans can sometimes fail. Since the Subprime Crisis, we should all be aware that private finance firms can go bankrupt, and so can corporate pension plans. If you're unaware of this, read up on Enron and the thousands of employees who lost their pension plans stuffed with Enron shares. Relying only on your corporate 401(k), private IRA or insurance product is a risk and should discourage you to get complacent about your financial future. The whole product range of private pension solutions is a vast field. It's your responsibility to be informed about the details of each scheme, financial service, and specific retirement product in your own country. For more details, see the recommended reading list at the end of this chapter, and consult with your local consumer protection agency.

Do You Need to Be Invested?

Another characteristic of private plans is that they often involve investing in the stock market; for many 401(k)s, that is what the account is structured *to do*. Instead of asking whether defined contribution plans are good or bad, a more important question to ask is whether we need to invest in stocks and mutual funds at all. The truth is that there is no academic evidence that we need to be invested in risky stocks or mutual funds. On the contrary, there are two fundamental reasons why you should stay away completely.

1. You know you can't and don't want to handle the possible psychological agony and the real financial consequences related to financial markets.
2. You have neither the knowledge nor the experience in financial market investing.

Ask yourself, how you would react to see your retirement portfolio reduced by 30% or more due to a blip in the market, even if your retirement is yet decades away. Can you trust yourself to stay the course? How much are you able and willing to lose? If the answer is "not much," then it's only prudent to make a conscious decision to stay away completely from any financial market product. Keep in mind the answer to this question is not purely mathematical— you need to understand what sort of an impact price declines and real losses will have on your life and your psychology. However, people aren't weak. To the contrary, we have built-in panic reflexes precisely to warn us when things are going wrong. Ignoring your instincts and reflexes may make sense in some settings; but in others, it makes none at all.

There are only two logical choices:

1. Stay away from Wall Street's money game entirely and focus on the traditional ways of preparing for retirement,

which includes not planning for retirement at all—the "default" position.

2. Study investing and its principles in detail and choose an appropriate strategy that suits your personality and God-given talents—the "optional" position. How do we move forward?

Default Asset: Cash is King

The best risk management policy in the world is to avoid unnecessary risks. If you don't understand the games; don't want to spend the time to learn them; and don't want to let other gamblers play with your money, eliminate risk by not participating in the game. If you know yourself, and have a strong distaste for all things Wall Street or simply can't stand the confusing nature of price auctions and price quotations, say, "No, thanks."

Don't despair. There are plenty of ways to get you prepared the old-fashioned way. And contrary to today's definition of saving for retirement, it all starts with good old cash. The absolute default position of any retirement plan or investing mission is always the least risky asset—and that is, by default, cash. Granted, it doesn't yield anything, and it will lose in value the longer you keep it dormant, but that is never an excuse to gamble or to be forced into a decision one will later regret.

What it means is to put your money aside, a portion of any paycheck or income you earn. There are so many personal finance books that teach how to save money, so I will not go into detail here. Some of the advice is sheer borderline insanity, and there seems to be heated discussions and conflicting positions on how to spend your money. However, it works; and that saving is a viable path to wealth accumulation is demonstrated by Mr. Money Moustache, a popular personal finance blogger. "If you can save 50% of your take-home pay starting at age 20, you'll be wealthy enough to retire by age 37," he argues.[42]

With this comes another core advantage: the *optionality* of cash. This is just a fancy way of saying that cash gives you more options than investments. If you have cash your money is easily accessible; you can buy what you like when you like it. You should not take this option lightly or for granted. No bank, professional portfolio manager, or even pension management has it; neither do full-time professional gamblers, day traders, and speculators. Controlling your cash and cash inflows is an enormous advantage to have.

The issue of fighting inflation remains. To compensate for this, keep your money in the highest quality short-term debt papers and government guaranteed debt notes, especially short term durations (not longer than a year) to avoid pricing risks. Through 401K or IRA plans, one could keep cash through high-quality money market funds that charge the least fees. The small income they generate could at least partially offset the risk of inflation while keeping market pricing risk low and liquidity high.

If you have access to Treasury Inflation-Protected Securities (TIPS), you should consider adding them to your retirement accounts. TIPS are extremely low-risk investments since they are backed by the U.S. government and the principle is inflation adjusted. According to TreasuryDirect, a website run by the Bureau of the Fiscal Service under the United States Department of the Treasury, "The principal of a TIPS increases with inflation and decreases with deflation, as measured by the Consumer Price Index. When a TIPS matures, you are paid the adjusted principal or original principal, whichever is greater."[43]

In today's low-interest rate and inflation environment, their yields are low, but that might change quickly. In 2017, Federal Reserve Chairwoman Janet Yellen increased benchmark rates by 25 basis points twice, and most experts expect her to increase them by another 25 basis points later in 2017. Long-term yields have already reacted to this by showing a rising uptrend. Two-year Treasury notes yield 1.4% per year in June 2017, the highest yield in eight years.

It's never a bad idea to keep a portion of your net worth in gold. General recommendations range from 5 to 10% with an emphasis on real physical gold, such as standard coins and bars. Gold has proven the test of time, not as an investment, but as insurance for your existing wealth. It's a very liquid and broad market, and you can always sell it for a fair price. Surprisingly, in the age of digital currencies, gold has additional benefits. As James Rickard, famed author of *the Road to Ruin*, asserts: "You can't hack it, you can't erase it, you can't delete it."[44]

The greatest advantage you have with this default option is simplicity and robustness. What you see is what you get. It's easy to manage, usually comes at minimum fees, and you can always keep a close watch over how much you have. You will not be bothered by the constant fear of stock markets crashing, needing to chase the latest hot tip, or Wall Street stealing from orphans. You can focus on the tasks you are good at. Choosing the simple way of simply stashing your money will never give you a misguided sense of security based on unrealistic growth assumptions. If there is not enough money you will know in advance, and will be forced to make proper adjustments that reinforce positive action. You either work longer, find new job opportunities beyond retirement age, or simply save more, when you can.

The Challenges of Saving

People's behavior about saving and investing can be pretty baffling. Richard Thaler and Cass Sunstein describe a puzzling case in their book *Nudge: Improving Decisions About Health, Wealth, and Happiness*. In the United Kingdom, some pension plans are paid entirely by the employer. To be eligible, all the employee has to do is visit HR and sign a document. That is literally *all* they have to do to get a pension without any contributions or pay deductions from their side. The fact that *one out of every two* eligible employees failed to sign up surprised the HR departments and Thaler and his research team. According to Thaler, it is "equivalent to not bothering to cash your paycheck." The only persuasive explanation they could come up with was "many people make poor financial decisions that cause themselves real financial harm."[45] It's the sad reality, but not a satisfying explanation.

Conversely, when the decision is, to a certain extent, taken out of our hands, the results can be impressive. Singapore is the perfect example. The Central Provident Fund in Singapore (CPFS), which is a compulsory employment based savings plan to fund retirement, healthcare and housing needs in Singapore, is one of the most successful savings plans in the world. Since its inauguration, the mandatory savings rate for both employers and employees was continuously set higher until it reached 25% in 1985 which applies to this day for employees.[vi] According to the Singapore Business Review, the bulk of household assets is in properties (49% of total), while cash and deposits made up 19% in 2013.[46] Additionally, according to Forbes, Singapore is the world's third richest country per capita.

How Much is Enough?

The biggest question of all- how much is enough? The conventional advice given by such firms as Fidelity Investments states that you should "have the equivalent of your salary saved by age 30 and (...) 9 times your final salary in savings, if you wanted to retire by age 65."[47] If you earned $50,000 by age 29, you would have put aside $50,000 by age 30. A person age 35 earning $70,000 a year is supposed to have saved $140,000 on monthly savings of $1,000, made up of matching contributions and private savings. If your salary were to be $120,000 gross by age 60, you would need have at least $1.1 million put aside at the time of your retirement at age 65.

There are so many assumptions in these calculations that it's impossible explore them all. Ask yourself: if you are 35 and receive

---

[vi] The employer's contribution was later reduced to 10% due to a recession.

$70,000 gross salary, what are the odds you will actually have up to $140,000 saved?

Many retirement calculations are based on the 4% withdrawal rule made famous by a 1998 study known as the Trinity Study[vii]. It suggests you can withdraw 4% of your account annually and never run out of money (assuming, of course, that your money earns more than 4% above the rate of current inflation—so, these days, roughly 7% in the US). In a popular blog post, business consultant and serial entrepreneur Tim Connelly wrote: "Under the 4% withdrawal rule you might have to save up $2 million to have a comfortable withdrawal rate [of] $50,000, not accounted for any inflation or tax scenario...totally passive index funds or bonds must save a minimum of $2,500,000."[48]

There's no doubt that this is profoundly challenging. It's obvious that you either need to jazz up the returns on your savings or, as the *Economist* has suggested, settle for a life of continuous work. Both options are less than enticing, even though Fidelity and Co. are more than happy to help out. Maybe there is a third way that utilizes the power of investing but doesn't rely on the help of financial service providers.

[vii] Trinity study is an informal name used to refer to an influential 1998 paper by three professors of finance at Trinity University.[1] It is one of a category of studies that attempt to determine "safe withdrawal rates"

Recommended Reading

- Thaler, Richard and Sunstein, Cass. *Nudge: Improving Decisions About Health, Wealth, and Happiness* by Richard Thaler and Cass Sunstein (Penguin Books).
- Collins, JL. *The Simple Path to Wealth: Your road map to financial independence and a rich, free life.* Jlcollinsnh.com. (CreateSpace Independent Publishing Platform; 1 edition June 18, 2016)

CHAPTER 5

SAILING THE INVESTMENT OCEAN

Investing is often described as the process of laying out money now in the expectation of receiving more money in the future. The whole process is similar to farming. You sow the seeds in the appropriate season, and wait for the crops to be harvested in the future. Both require planning, hard work, and an understanding of the effects of time. In farming, you can cover your bases by diversifying crops for different seasons, or by choosing crops that yield the highest calorie output for calorie input.

A successful investment formula looks rather simple. You establish a primary cash flow. You start saving part of that cash flow, which you reinvest, or purchase valuables that increase or at least maintain value that you could sell later. It's all about future cash flows that result from the decisions we make today. In the process, you enjoy an effect that financial gurus call 'compounding of returns'—in other words, making more money with money at an exponential rate. This is the core attraction of investing, and the main reason to take the time to learn it from the ground up. Just imagine if your income from past investments is enough to cover all your everyday costs. This is pure financial freedom—the freedom to do what you really want in life, to be the person you are striving to be.

In 1968, legendary money manager Gerald Tsai described why he felt at home in the world of investing in the center of Manhattan: "I felt that being a foreigner I didn't have a competitive disadvantage there." Indeed, the skill of investing skill is a powerful tool that doesn't discriminate. Successful investors are everywhere and are different ages, races, genders, and socio-economic classes. You could be a black woman from Detroit and become an investment success, like Latasha Kinard from Millennial Wealth Academy, or a German-born, gay, white male, like Peter Thiel.

The Joys of Passive Income

The ultimate goal of investing is, of course, passive income. By definition, passive income means *acquiring income without actively producing it*. There is nothing more powerful than the prospect of passive income. If done correctly, mastering investing has some very attractive benefits, which include more money, potential early retirement, the removal of the chains of an unloved 9 to 5 job, and the escape of the burden of 100-hour shifts at consultancy, investment banks or law firms. Passive income could mean the ability to live out your hedonistic tendencies as Hedonismbot encourages, "apologize for nothing."[49] For others, it means dedicating life to study, self-improvement, and/or community welfare.

Another advantage of investing skills is the possibility of location independence, or a Location Independent Lifestyle Design (LILD). The original idea behind LILD was, as Timothy Ferriss described in his book *The Four Hour Work Week*, to escape spending your day in a cubicle doing menial or unfulfilling work. Put simply, it is "not being tied to a certain location for any reason."[50] It is much more than just changing working from the beach with your laptop, although this idea appeals to many readers. It means making a conscious decision to be in control of your life for "maximizing your lifetime experience of happiness."[51] As opposed to early retirement, LILD practitioners still pursue paid activities. It could be the skilled IT expert, a specialist for SEO (Search Engine Optimization) and digital marketing, who offers his or her skills as a freelancer working from a coworking space in Bali. It could be the yoga instructor who gives online lessons and seminars via YouTube or Skype while improving his or her skills in an ashram somewhere in India. It could be the fiction writer renting a castle in the remote areas of Transylvania that really gets his or her creatives juices flowing while co-writing with other authors at the same location and sharing the cost of renting the castle.

What all these examples have in common is the advantages of earning their revenues in a hard currency—such as USD or EUR—while living in a country with a lower value currency such as Poland, Vietnam or Mexico. This alone can reduce the cost of living noticeably. Many creatives, as part of growing group of *digital nomads*, can still enjoy the same result and the same standard of living they'd enjoy back home in the industrialized West. They simply utilize telecommunication technologies to earn a living wherever they choose to reside for the moment. But it's not only the financial aspect that has real merits. Those not comfortable with extreme weather and seasonal changes simple escape to a climate zone that is more suitable for their well-being. Like birds changing location with seasons, they, too, can change their work locations for a couple of months and exploit the best the world has to offer. This is real location independent lifestyle design.

It's obvious LILD is much easier to attain than a strict form of early retirement, since you would still be working. In fact, LILD could be the smooth transitioning period from full-time employment to retirement. In many cases, those who have already achieved financial freedom and location independence continue pursuing their work activities. Many times, their lifestyle is founded on the passion for their work that made them a financial success in the first place. From own observations, even those who could afford early retirement continue some sort of work activity. LILD is your *choice* to make, and you will never have to make a decision under pressure.

Doing it wrong: learning from the fat cats.

If you plan for retirement the conventional way, you will hear of mutual funds, index funds and mutual fund compositions—the whole befuddling kaboodle known as "asset allocation." You might also have heard of "risk diversification" and "dollar cost averaging" (and if you haven't, I've provided you with a description in the appendix). Investment approaches have been in place at least since 1981. However, Tony Robbins convincingly demonstrated that buying a bunch of mutual funds and hiring financial advisers are inefficient. John Bogle concurs, "The system has disproportionately profited the mutual fund industry and left their clients hanging." Those trying to aim for above market returns never beat their indexes, and the return expectation for indexes are about 4 to 5% going forward.

A logical choice is to search and study those who are already wealthy. After all, they must have done *something* right. Naturally, you would study the wealthiest families in the world. You will instantly notice that they either are the largest land and property owners, or own businesses, or have a combination of both where one finances the other and vice versa. They possess gold and extensive art collections accumulated over generations. They are usually considered old money—like the Rockefellers, Hindujas, or Toyodas. You can also read up on new billionaires like Jeff Bezos of Amazon, Warren Buffett of Berkshire Hathaway or George Soros the billionaire financier and former hedge fund manager. Certainly, they have all great lessons to teach.

For example, this particular group did not achieve their wealth by handing their money to Wall Street on a silver platter. On the contrary, they have been using financial markets as an additional tool in their repertoire of wealth creation or preservation, but never as the core of their wealth. And they most certainly didn't achieve their fortunes by praying every day that everything would play out as economists and experts predicted. The wealthy usually follow a much more pragmatic approach, by aiming for returns that compensate for the risk taken and avoiding unnecessary risks altogether.

That being said, we can actually learn more from figuring out what we *can't* do that these people *can*. In other words, if we look closer, we can see their current reality of success can't be replicated by us. Paradoxically, figuring this out contains a valuable lesson in itself.

Don't Do as The Fat Cats Do

Here's an interesting fact: If the top 10 wealthiest people on the planet could grow their assets at a rate of 15% per year or more, they'd control all the wealth of the entire planet in no time.[52] If Bill Gates made 4% after tax on his $89.2 billion fortune in 2017, that would mean an increase of $3.6 billion, even after one year of doing nothing. Warren Buffett amused himself in one of his letters to shareholders, by explaining the absurd implications of ever higher compound growth rates:

> "Carl Sagan has entertainingly described this phenomenon, musing about the destiny of bacteria that reproduce by dividing into two every 15 minutes. Says Sagan: "That means four doublings an hour, and 96 doublings a day. Although a bacterium weighs only about a trillionth of a gram, its descendants, after a day of wild asexual abandon, will collectively weigh as much as a mountain...in two days, more than the sun - and before very long, everything in the universe will be made of bacteria." Not to worry, says Sagan: Some obstacle always impedes this kind of exponential growth. "The bugs run out of food, or they poison each other, or they are shy about reproducing in public."[53]

He goes on:

"We face another obstacle: In a finite world, high growth rates must self-destruct. If the base from which the growth is taking place is tiny, this law may not operate for a time. But when the base balloons, the party ends: A high growth rate eventually forges its own anchor."

The point is, wealthy people can and have to be satisfied with lower returns for their wealth, because they are coming from a totally different vantage point. They live in very different return reality than we normal folks do. In fact, seeking out the kind of high returns you should be aiming for makes no economic sense to them; the economies, in which they function, simply can't sustain it. But, that doesn't mean you have to accept their return reality as your own. In fact, until they got super rich, neither did they accept a low-return reality. They too initially enjoyed very high compound returns early on in their wealth career. Warren Buffett achieved average returns of 30% for his early partnerships back in the 1950s and 60s. Today, he still achieves above market returns, but nothing compares to his early days as a money manager. Those who are wealthy today didn't achieve their wealth through aiming for market returns in stock markets. They either got wealthy through exponential growth of their underlying businesses, their unique talents, or a combination of them both, which often included a form of financial leverage. Most celebrated hedge fund managers didn't get rich through the returns they achieved within their funds, but through the fees they charge their clients as operational managers of such funds.

So, instead of copying the fat cats, you should be doing the *exact opposite* of what they do today. For example, the super-rich and billion dollar asset managers never create assets from scratch, they buy other people's assets for their specific investment requirements and strategies to maintain their wealth. It's just not a prudent use of their time to set up business operations from scratch. Creating a startup company worth $1 million or even $10 million that could take many months or even years to achieve profitability is just not a prudent use of their time if they could buy existing assets at $1 billion or more tomorrow. A 10 million dollar company is not even that single drop of water in the vast Sahara desert for a person as Bill Gates. As Warren Buffett says himself—deals of this size don't move his "needle" in term of performance to the bottom line of Berkshire Hathaway. But as I will show, this is precisely what you should be doing—and, in fact, it is what all these colossal investors did at the beginning themselves.

The ultra-rich can also afford to play the capital markets in an entirely different way to you. Whereas wealthy people might have the freedom to overpay for assets, due to their lower return expectations to start with and huge pots of money, individual investors don't have that luxury. If you lost $10 billion out of your $40 billion fortune, it certainly hurts, but you will survive. A person who loses $10,000 from a $40,000 retirement savings is a totally different story. Through the media, we are overexposed to the deals and trading done in financial markets as an easy way of creating wealth. But what has this to do with investing for the common folks? All this should mean nothing to you. Again, we should do the exact opposite of what they (wealthy) do in order to achieve high compound returns—stay away from capital markets, at least until we join their ranks.

Recommended Reading List

- Ferriss, Timothy. *The 4-Hour Workweek: Escape 9-5, Live Anywhere, and Join the New Rich Hardcover* (Harmony; Exp Upd edition December 15, 2009).
- *Graham, Benjamin, The Intelligent Investor: A Book of Practical Counsel* (Harper & Row Publisher 1986 edition).

CHAPTER 6
ALL ENGINES GO!

Investing skills have the potential to solve the retirement riddle. Their benefits are enormous—ranging from early retirement to location independence and the power to shape your own life, instead of being shaped by it. Before you continue, you will need to acknowledge two simple truths about investing:

1. *All investing involves risk*, and hence, includes elements of gambling.
2. Making decisions about money *is as much a subliminal decision-making process as it is a rational process.*

The bottom line is that when making decisions about money, we base our decisions on incomplete data, which inevitably brings in the element of chance. Furthermore, we are constantly influenced by powerful cognitive biases, especially when it comes to money. You need to be aware that there will be forces that will test your resolve. The biggest tests of them all lie in devastating market crashes and in adverse economic developments such as prolonged recessions.

Furthermore, there are two further challenges in the investing process that pose insurmountable hurdles for many students of investing:

1. How to generate the money for investing
2. How to invest productively

As we've seen, existing models are prey to a combination of very low returns, exposure to uncertain inflation and tax changes, financial turmoil, and over-exposure to human errors. On top of this, there is this constant struggle with a whole array of industry-insider parasites and leeches the high concentration of money attracts. What is most perplexing is that conventional models never deal with the question of where the money to invest actually comes from, and what the reliability of that source should be. In my opinion, this is one of the most important aspects of long-term investment success. Conventional models for retirement planning just assume the money is there with an endless stream of more cash coming in. So what is the solution?

It's clear a very different approach to investing and retirement planning is necessary, and its key requirements must be:

- To approach the two aforementioned challenges from the bottom up.
- To understand risk and return, and to consistently demand high returns for the real risks we take.
- To understand the psychological consequences, and to minimize and avoid cognitive biases.
- To follow more suitable role models and to do the exact opposite of the very wealthy

In this chapter, I will discuss investing challenge #1 and how to overcome it. Then, I'll illustrate my point with three case studies. In the subsequent chapter, I will be discussing an investment approach very different to what you read in conventional finance books. In both, I will provide a proper introduction to investing.

Please keep in mind that this is not a specific *how to manual*, though it has elements of it. It is more an introduction to an alternative—in my view, a superior—approach to retirement, retirement planning and investing.[54]

Challenge I: Solving the Chicken and Egg problem

How can you invest if you don't have money? How can you have money if you can't invest in the first place? Well, the short answer is—through leveraging your existing resources, and continuously "leveling up."

All humans have one resource: time. Investing starts early, when you decide how to spend your time—watching TV, hanging out, drinking beer in front of the local gas station, honing your skills at the local gym, or establishing your online media presence. It's your choice! But keep in mind that all investing starts with *the first* cash engine that supplies cash for all your future investments, and that is the first and most important investment in *ourselves*—the *primary cash engine*.

What is a Cash Engine?

Put simply, a cash engine is a series of activities that efficiently convert time and effort into cash. There are different types and sizes of cash engines, but once an engine is set up, there's not much you need to do except to keep it ticking along. Like any engine, cash engines will suffer from wear and tear, and need maintenance. Inevitably, they will conk out. But while they're ticking along, you can happily step aside and promote yourself to a supervisory role, and enjoy what is essentially *passive income*.

The *conventional* path to your primary cash engines is to go straight into employment after many years of education. Many professions require less time input, but some take years. For example, it is often said that a medical doctor, after years of training and practice, will eventually become a high earner. The same counts for other highly specialized professions such as lawyers, architects or academic professionals. These are all well-respected forms of establishing a primary source of income, but they come with their own disadvantages.

Any high-earning profession requires sacrifices and constant input. Once you secure your employment, what follows are years of average market salaries, office gossip, and politics to scramble for the few privileged position within an organization. Furthermore, if you don't work, you don't get paid. The machine stops running.

This phenomenon applies to all forms of employment, that require you to show up. Real passive income looks different, even though many employed might intuitively follow Wooden Allen's advice "Showing up is 80 percent of life." Traditional employment will always have its limitations. There is a ceiling on how much one person can earn in their respective field. We may get laid-off, or we may be forcibly retired. Self-employment is naturally limited to the hours you can put in each day. After all, you can't make a carbon copy of yourself.

Hence, relying on one single cash engine for the rest of your life is a rather risky proposition, and based on many expert's forecasts, the financial risks inherent in such a one-sided model will only increase over time. The "UBER Economy," "FinTech," and "Robot Revolution" are just a few buzz words that swirl around these days—and all represent trends that are picking up momentum. Pretty soon, you, like the rest of us, could see yourself and your most valuable investments' value wane into nothing. You have reached a crossroads. While you have achieved regular income through traditional employment or even self-employment, through many years of personal sacrifices at school and college, the path to retirement has just started. It is now up to you to make a vital decision about how you continue investing your limited resources of time and money. You can choose the path your parents followed or choose a very different path.

Diversification Where it Counts

Escaping some of the more gloomy forecasts basic risk management in form of crude diversification is a valid solution. The trick is to diversify into additional cash engines to reduce the dependence on one single cash engine at any time. The reasons for such an approach is commonsensical. Two money makers are always better than one. Besides being less dependent on a single income source, the power of compounding can really show its effects when you have several cash flows running, (provided you can keep your spending under control), and reinvest some of the cash back into your platform. From a practical point of view, any additional cash engine requires a building and testing phase. Like engineering a real mechanical machine, you want to be able to test it before you can rely on it. Preparing for additional cash engines early on takes away this pressure. It's fair to ask how we can achieve that, if you have your hands full with your daily job, whether you are employed or self-employed.

The key to creating a secondary cash engines is *bootstrapping*.

Bootstrapping has mainly been used in the computer world when describing "a self-starting process that is supposed to proceed without external input." In business bootstrapping means "starting a business without external help or capital. Such startups fund the development of their company through internal cash flow, and are cautious with their expenses."[55] It fits perfectly into Nassim Taleb's risk averse investment strategy, which makes use of asymmetric risk reward outcomes. If your bootstrapped bet pays off, it pays off exponentially and over long periods of time. If it doesn't, very little financial resources are lost but valuable experiences are gained that can be utilized for any type of employment activity.

So, How do You Bootstrap?

Well, first, you will have to overcome the mental hurdles of creating new cash engines from scratch. Never forget that most of us have experience in establishing a cash engine already—our primary cash engine, described above. You rarely start from zero, and any form of education and training are invaluable in helping you move forward. Everything you've learned, both academic and practical, will stand you in good stead for when you strike out on your own.

Next, is to make the very symbolic first step - a baby step in terms of effort or even financial input - but the most important you can make. Today, setting up a simple internet-based business might cost you less than $1,000. With each dollar you invest, and each hour you spend building, you are able to increase the chances of financial success, like a LEGO building that grows with each block.

And like LEGO, there are endless variations of how you could build your cash engine. There are no fixed rules nor set pass. That is one of its key benefits. It depends more on your character and your personal preference on how you approach bootstrapping and how profitable each decision will be. It could be selling books, art, or music to online consultancy and training courses. The range of possible products and services is as wide as our economy. All you have to invest is a small amount of your available cash and a lot of your time. For example, a doctor could write books or create podcasts on his particular subject. He would enjoy the benefit of selling more of his services or products. Accountants could provide valuable accounting tips and advice, and hence, find new customers and buyers for their accounting services that could open up consulting opportunities much later in their careers. Even those without specialized training, e.g. in typical blue or white-collar jobs can find financial success in their own passions. It could be the video-game aficionado who creates YouTube videos with live commentary or the sci-fi fan who produces an entire series of their own sci-fi stories. It could be the housewives who is into cute toys and has created toys of her own design. These rather unique skills and passions can be monetized in just the same way any vocational training can be.

If you don't have any passions now, you can develop them over time, by trying out several things and consulting with people you respect and admire. After all, you do have almost 40 years to come up with something. Once you have zeroed in on one potential idea, keep in mind that your additional cash engine might not turn a profit quickly, and your out of pocket spending accumulates for the first months even years. It will test your patience and your resolve, when you spend money without immediate rewards. But keep in mind, that bootstrapping your cash engine would never require enormous initial outlays or large financial commitments. By investing small amounts of your own money this approach to investing could never financially bankrupt you. On the contrary, you would learn every valuable lesson about true investing. The whole process of establishing passive income through several small investments in your own cash engine will train you to become a better investor, capable of identifying true asymmetric bets. Each financial decision you make becomes part of a learning process of understanding financial risks and rewards.

It doesn't have to stop here. As soon as you have your first additional cash engine running, you're free to establish another independently working cash engine or optimize your existing cash engines. Whatever you choose will add to your bottom line and create more asymmetric bets in the process. In the end, you will have established a platform with parallel running cash engines that produce cash day after day. You will have created your own powerful cash engine *platform* that will give you the operational basis of financial strength for all your future investment endeavors, including your first forays into Wall Street.

THE ADVANTAGES

Higher Compounding Rates

Establishing your own cash engines promises very high returns on invested capital that can generate a very powerful *compounding effect*. To demonstrate its earnings power, let's assume the entire cost of producing your own first novel costs $2,000. In due course, it becomes an Amazon best-seller and makes $20,000 for several years in a row. In the first year, you would have made 900% on your invested capital with similar returns for the following years until profits fade away. However, in the process, you will have reinvested most of the profits of the first book into more novels or writing projects. This, in turn, will generate more cash flows that again could be reinvested in more projects, hence creating a powerful profit cycle upwards. As a result, you will have created a cash engine from scratch that can absorb more money while still producing high returns year after year.

What I just described is known in financial terms as *compound interest*. It's defined as "interest computed on the sum of an original principal and accrued interest."[56] In other words, compound interest is the addition of interest to the initial money invested, so that the next interest payout will be even higher. The rate of return might be the same, but the actual money paid out after the second year will be higher. It's known as "interest on interest." It is the result of reinvesting interest, rather than paying it out. Naysayers would quickly point out that I didn't account for the endless hours of writing and producing the books. That's true. The question would be how much value you would assign to an hour spent writing your book. If you do it in your free time, its value could *de facto* be zero. You are leveraging your free resource - time.

All financial experts would agree on the importance of compounding money. In fact, it's one of their main arguments for investing in index or mutual funds. Proponents of conventional

Wall Street investing just love to talk about it as the easy route to riches. The catch is, that their touted compound rates are so low that compounding loses all its effectiveness. Worse, their idea of compounding money through stock market investing is so inconsistent and sporadic compounding could even turn *negative*. If you fed these models more realistic contemporary compound rates on savings and investments of around three percent, you might be lucky enough to break even in thirty or forty years, thanks to inflation and tax considerations.

In stark contrast, your personal cash engines promise much higher and many times more consistent compound returns than anything you could ever imagine receiving from mutual funds or any other form of conventional investing these days.

The reasons for higher returns are simple. In a way it's like cooking your own meals rather than eating out. If you eat out, you will always have to pay a premium for the fact that someone else has done the work for you. However, if you learn how to cook your own meals, you'll not only be able to do it *just the way you like*, but it'll be cheaper. In effect, you are not sharing your potential profit margin with anyone, but keeping all the benefits for yourself. If you decided to ever sell your favorite dish to the public, you would make sure to charge an appropriate price for all the training and cooking you had done the years before. We all know that there is no free lunch!

Buying other people's assets works on the same principles. No clear-minded person, who has a winning formula for sale, would undercharge a potential buyer. More likely than not, any potential buyer can count on being overcharged, and that's only natural. If you considered the inefficiencies of pricing mechanisms, whether in private or public transactions, combined with the gullibility of many potential buyers, you can see that room for error, on both sides, is there. Be sure that you are the person who is in control of overcharging others or keeping the profits for yourself.

Higher Reinvestment Rates

Creating cash engines encourages higher savings rates in the form of reinvestments into your existing cash platform. The whole process of creating something from scratch has a much more tangible and rewarding character than hoping for some indefinite rewards in 30 or 40 years time. You see the effects of your redeployed money right in front of your eyes. The whole process of saving and reinvesting money from your earnings is a highly visible and tangible process that creates positive behavioral change. The conventional way of saving and investing for retirement just can't offer this. When you pay someone else to do it for you, you are completely taking out of the most vital process - making the decisions that count.

Superior Risk Management

The topic of "diversification" is never far from discussions of risk. How many books and even Nobel-prize winning papers have been published on the topic of diversification![57] But with all these demands of sophisticated risk diversification, a lot of experts seem to forget one vital point: If you lost your job, and you are forced to liquidate your investment portfolio out of financial need, the best asset allocation models and the best-diversified portfolio wouldn't be of much use. In other words, real diversification starts elsewhere.

There is a reason why dual-income couples feel more financially secure than single-income families. If one spouse loses his or her job, the other partner can pick up the slack. It's elementary risk diversification at the very source. The same principle applies to having a diversified cash-engine platform. The chances that all cash engines fail at the same time is very low. Hence, it's the most efficient form of financial diversification.

Another reason why this form of risk management is superior to existing models is the quality of investment decisions. In addition to being the master of your financial destiny, carefully selected cash engines are the perfect fit for a risk management technique made famous by former hedge fund manager and best-selling author Nassim Taleb. As he puts it:

> "If you put 90 percent of your funds in boring cash (assuming you are protected from inflation) or something called a "numeraire repository of value," and 10 percent in very risky, maximally risky, securities, you cannot possibly lose more than 10 percent, while you are exposed to massive upside. Someone with 100 percent in so-called "medium" risk securities has a risk of total ruin from the miscomputation of risks."[58]

In other words: hoard plenty of your wealth in liquid assets without regretting low returns, but add the benefits of asymmetrical bets. You don't need to religiously stick to his suggested 90% figure. You could do 80% or even as low as 50%, depending on how confident you feel with other types of investments. Whatever the percentage ratio is, the liquidity reserve has three core functions:

1. Maintain your psychological well-being.
2. To give you liquidity in times of emergencies.
3. To give you firepower when you come along more asymmetric bets.

If you ever come across an outstanding opportunity that's an absolute no-brainer or basically free cash, make use of your liquidity reserves. Any additional cash engine will automatically lower the need for high liquidity reserves, as cash would be coming in on a monthly basis. It would give you plenty of cash reserves even if there were a catastrophic failure and all cash engines stopped running at the same time.

Last but by no means least, this new risk management approach would divert your attention from gambling and an intense focus on financial markets and price speculations. As a cash engine owner, you would always appreciate the *optionality of cash* and the value of cash reserves. By default, you would always consider all your available options first and choose the investments that offer the best risk return rewards. If you tend to your cash engines first, you would soon realize that it would be foolish to put the money into stock markets. Why would you put your money into stocks where you could make 5% but lose 50%, at any time, without ever being in control? You usually get much higher returns from your own cash engine platform - returns you are in control of and risks you understand.

High Educational Value

Creating your own cash engines is highly educational. If you study Warren Buffett's early life, you can read up on how he began investing—he invested in his financial education, and then started creating his first cash engines. He delivered newspapers, then invested his savings in a pinball machine and a beat up Rolls Royce that he rented out. At age 15, he bought 40 acres of farmland in Omaha, Nebraska from his savings. It must have been a great feeling, and a great experience collecting and holding each penny. But, I am sure he learned even more when no-one used his machines or rented his Rolls Royce or worse, when the machines broke down, and he had to spend time and money to fix them.

He admitted that his early experiences of entrepreneurship taught him valuable lessons for his future career in money management and investing. Many don't realize it, but Warren Buffett was always an owner of cash engines. When he returned to Omaha, Nebraska in 1956 after some formative years on Wall Street with his mentor and boss Benjamin Graham, he instantly created his famous Buffett Partnership (Buffett Associates Ltd). Eventually, his partnership structure fed into Berkshire Hathaway, and the rest is history. Today, he sits at the helm of possibly the most powerful cash engine platform the world has ever seen.

Hence, establishing your cash engines would teach you a core idea of investing. You would learn the concepts of economics, not from a textbook's abstract formulas and graphs, but through real applications that affect your bottom line instantly. You would instantly understand such vital concepts of supply and demand, and its importance to economic price determination. You would understand the concept of cause and effect and input/output ratios. In other words, if you are lazy couch potato nothing would ever happen and your personal success is directly correlated with your own efforts and determination to succeed. You would learn the impact of economic cycles on your own financial situation and how you could make yourself less prone to adverse economic developments. You would truly understand the magic of compounding returns, because you could see the magic happening right in front of you.

If you are still not convinced, consider the free crash course in simple accounting and budgeting. You would instantly understand the difference between real cash flows, i.e. cash hitting your bank accounts vs. accounting earnings, money just on paper. You would learn everything about modern marketing and promotional techniques in order to generate sales. At the very least, you would become aware of the elaborate techniques luring *you* to buy things and, like Dr. Zoidberg, you would finally become a crafty consumer.

Satisfaction

There is one more key benefit to this approach; it's more than just money. Nothing is better than the feeling of satisfaction when overcoming obstacles. My mother has been a housewife all her life. She raised four kids, and when we all left home to lead our own lives, she was left alone and without a purpose.

She needed a new life calling and found it in a local charity that supported children from the region that suffered from the immediate fall out of the Chernobyl disaster at the border between

Ukraine and Belarus. In order to raise funds for these kids, she started an import business. She became so successful that her enterprising activity alone was able to stem most of the financial burden of these charity projects. She did all this, with a high school degree, and no knowledge about technology or business management.

Initially, I didn't understand her passion and energy. I couldn't understand her countless nights of preparation. She had to get up early in the mornings to organize, to lead, and to whip her team into shape (that included me). Only later did I realize that she gained satisfaction and pride in what she was doing that would make her overcome even the fiercest resistance towards old notions and some deep-rooted prejudices. She found a new calling, and she made it work.

THE DOWNSIDES

The idea of cash engines is neither new nor perfect. It's not meant to be an "all weather" solution for everyone. As mentioned in chapter 5, for the ultra-rich, starting new cash engines from scratch makes little economic sense. For the average individual, that shouldn't be a problem. Even if you had millions in net worth, cash engines would still be a fertile ground for growing your wealth at much higher rates than nearly any other method. But having said this, there are also many downsides and disadvantages.

Financial Risks

I have already mentioned the financial risks. These are limited to the amount of money you put in. If you give up midway, the money spent until this point might be lost. But since you can bootstrap most simple cash engines with minimal amounts, the process will never bankrupt you.[viii] However, if you borrowed money—on your credit card, from friends and family, or even from banks—your financial risks grow exponentially. From a person who receives compound interest, you quickly degenerate into a person who pays compound interest. Building cash engines on borrowed money is not a good idea, and should be avoided unless you have some experience and feel comfortable managing financial leverage. In any case, as the main character of bootstrapping cash engines relies on leveraging existing resources rather than finance, the real risks lie somewhere else.

[viii] Not considering any legal risks if you break the law - particular consideration should be given to copyright law, personal tax filings and issues related to legal entities.

Opportunity Cost

Building cash engines from scratch takes time. Setting up systems and procedures so that money automatically flows into your pockets takes time. Proponents of conventional investing quantify the value of time as 'opportunity cost'—a cost that symbolizes what you could have gained if you followed the path of purchasing mutual funds or other popular retirement products and, with the time saved, done something else. Some would say that the time it takes to build up your cash engines could have made you market returns or risk-free returns from US Treasury Notes.

Be under no illusion that starting a cash engine takes time. There are the endless hours you will have to spend during work weeks (for many before or after work) or the countless weekends you will have to sacrifice testing websites and writing content or sales letters. Missing time with friends and family is not a sacrifice everyone is willing to make. Are you prepared to give up your precious free time?

Frustration

Finally, it can be pretty damn hard. It's certainly not as simple as opening an account at Vanguard or Fidelity. Without effort, nothing will happen. Furthermore, creating cash engines from scratch requires a certain amount of patience. You will face frustration—the frustration of working hard for a long time while not seeing immediate financial rewards; the frustration of unexpected mishaps, self-caused or caused blunders by third parties; the frustration of feeling dumb because of technical issues that make you want to smash your keyboard or even your entire laptop. Take it from a person who went through all of it, there will be days when the frustration grows so intense you feel sick to your stomach, and you want to give up.

Additionally, there is always the issue of luck. Some people are simply lucky enough to come up with the right idea at the right time for the right market. Many others fail due to just one bad decision. Be aware that this may happen. The whole point of bootstrapping cash engines is that even if this comes to pass, it won't mean your financial ruin. Steel yourself, get up, and grab the next opportunity, knowing that you have nothing to lose.

Recommended Reading

- Pearson, Taylor. *The End of Jobs: Money, Meaning and Freedom Without the 9-to-5* (Lioncrest Publishing; 1 edition June 29, 2015).
- Brunson, Russell. *Expert Secrets: The Underground Playbook for Finding Your Message, Building a Tribe, and Changing the World* (Morgan James Publishing June 6, 2017).
- Walling, Rob, "The Stairstep Approach to Bootstrapping," accessed July 1, 2017, http://www.softwarebyrob.com/2015/03/26/the-stairstep-approach-to-bootstrapping.
- Andrews, Dan, "The 1000 Day Rule: What Living the Dream Really Looks Like," accessed July 1, 2017, http://www.tropicalmba.com/living-the-dream.

CHAPTER 7
NEW ROLE MODELS

On of the biggest challenges of following the path of establishing your own cash engine platform is the lack of appropriate role models or the lack of awareness that there are many appropriate role models. As we already know, following Jeff Bezos, Mark Cuban or Oprah Winfrey may look easy, but there is only so much we can usefully take away from how they handle their portfolios.

I would like to introduce you to three case studies each representing a valuable lesson for people who are not already jillionaires, but have found their very own ways to handle the challenges of retirement planning. John Cavendish represents the classic case of someone who is traditionally employed while creating an additional cash engine on the side. Miles and Melanie Beckler show how teamwork and shared values can overcome even the largest hurdles and obstacles. And lastly, Travis Jamison demonstrates how far you can take the concept of cash-engine platforms when combined with traditional capital allocation methods.

JOHN CAVENDISH

The story of John Cavendish is a truly an inspiring story of how he transformed himself from a traditional white-collar worker to a 28-year-old, semi-retired, full-time manager of cash engines dedicated to traveling the world. He is an example of what's possible for those stuck in a 9 to 5 day job. As we shall see, for Cavendish, it was all about making a well-calculated move, tailored to his ambitions and capabilities.

Cavendish studied mechanical engineering at the University of Birmingham and graduated in 2011 with a Master's degree in mechanical engineering. He found a job, which required him to travel around the UK on various engineering projects. However, he soon discovered that his salary wasn't enough to enjoy a lifestyle he had in mind for himself, especially in big cities. He wanted to earn more, save more, and invest more.

Cavendish surmised that real wealth comes through business ownership and real estate ownership. Unfortunately, owning real estate was out of the question without over-leveraging himself. He would end up binding himself even deeper to his day job; thus, he decided to establish a business.

His action plan was very simple. First, he became a freelance contractor, doing mechanical engineering for more pay, which allowed him to save more money, in return for less social and retirement benefits. During his time as a contractor, he learned the ropes of taking responsibility for his own financial affairs, including budgeting and spending, as well as the self-initiative of gaining and managing his own work contracts.

His decision paid off. He quickly saved up cash while exploring his options. During this transitional period, he explored and tested several business models for himself, including content blogging, real estate and e-commerce. However, it wasn't all roses. In his own words, he "spent a year failing."

Eventually, he found something that appealed to him and was the right fit for his personality and ambitions. Thanks to continuous researching, lots of testing, and twists of fate, he decided to start an Amazon business. Why Amazon? According to him, he understood that Amazon is a business that, once all the relevant organization was done, "almost runs itself."59 Prior to taking the dive, he gambled on the fact that he was still contracting, and still a certified engineer. At worst, all he would lose was his starting capital of $5,000 and a bit of time. He quickly realized that certain products would sell better online than others. Selling an ebook for .99 cents or selling a physical product for $20, with equal demand, certainly makes a difference for sales and earnings growth. He quickly zoned in on the specific products that made economic sense for the UK market. He finally decided on the health and fitness supplements category and his decision would pay off in record time.

He understood that he needed to research the markets to whom he would sell his Amazon products. He compared the e-commerce markets in the US and the UK, and it was easy to recognize that e-commerce in the UK was still far behind the potential that the US had so impressively demonstrated. The UK was also far less crowded, and thus, an ideal place to launch his Amazon platform.

Within less than one and a half years, he achieved over a million dollars in sales, selling a range of health and training supplements —a market that is still growing to this day. More importantly, he had established his first self-running cash engine, bringing in cash outside his day job. Luck might have been involved, but his diligence, his inclination to use spreadsheets, logic, and simple math to come to better decisions—were all part of a winning formula. With just $5,000 and some effort, he'd set himself up for life.

His business took off, and he quit his contracting job to focus on building his cash engine platform full time. Through his growing network of fellow entrepreneurs, he gathered information concerning locations to maximize his earnings. He desired to create an environment for himself that would inspire and help him grow. He relocated to Ho Chi Minh City, Vietnam where he established his first operational base. The cost of living was much lower than in London, and his direct access to a vibrant community of like-minded people gave him the assurance that this was the right decision for him.

In Vietnam, for the first time, he was confronted with more money than he knew what to do with. He revisited his old dream of owning real estate investments. Whenever he visited family and friends in the UK, he would contact real estate agents and property owners. Eventually, he bought a small property to get a taste of real estate investing, but it wasn't what he expected. First, he recognized how flooded the UK market was with bidders who had easy access to easy money. Second, he noticed how low other real estate investor's return requirements were—4% or less on their real estate deals. Plus, they were not considering the financial risks taken when utilizing more and more financial leverage through complex mortgage contracts. He looked at the numbers and compared them to his Amazon business and the stellar compound returns he had achieved thus far. In the end, the decision was simple. He decided against investing in real estate, and to replicate his winning formula by establishing several more lines of Amazon business, each time making minor improvements and adjustments. Eventually, he decided to start an Amazon-related service for those wanting to learn about establishing Amazon businesses themselves. It was something he wished he had access to when he went through his trial and error phase.

It made sense to him, because his emails and feedback showed the demand was there. With a business associate, he launched a service leveraging their existing skills and collective experiences. The result was FBA Frontiers, a company that specifically helps US sellers take advantage of the potential that Amazon Europe offers. He added another cash engine to his platform with far better returns than he could ever hope for when investing in UK Real Estate.

Cavendish has been a full-time business owner and entrepreneur since September 2015. Today, he commutes between the UK and Vietnam several times a year. In his free time, he travels throughout Asia. He visits business partners in the Philippines, Thailand, and China, while exploring Bali, Chiang Mai and the cities of Europe. He leads a life that many of his peers from his university days could only dream of. He is a textbook example, of how a person with a college degree, on a path to a middle-class existence, can leverage themselves into a career as an entrepreneur with very different views on retirement. His exposure to project management and understanding systems helped him to establish his own cash engine platform. He seems to have a very controlled and systematic approach to decision-making, investing, and risk analysis.

One could assume that Cavendish has a personality for risk-taking. If you meet him in person, you may think otherwise. Far from being a gambler, he is, in his own words, "extremely risk averse." Yes, he took concentrated bets, but he intuitively understood the concept of the power of favorable risk/reward scenarios. Today, he manages several Amazon cash engines, and an Amazon-related service business training future Amazon sellers. He continues to accumulate cash waiting for new asymmetric bets he understands.

You should also note that he has a brokerage account and a couple of financial market investments, but they are minuscule compared to what he has in tangible and intangible assets through his business ownerships. For him, success is all about generating wealth.

MELANIE AND MILES BECKLER

Miles and Melanie Beckler are the perfect example of how cash-engine management and efficient risk diversification can work for married couples. They are a new generation of independent investors achieving very high compound return rates on their invested capital. Like John Cavendish, they took a very different road from their peers and achieved a unique form of early retirement in record time. Here is how they did it.

In my point of view, they have a perfect diversification model. Even if they completely stopped working, their cash engines would run on autopilot for a very long time. Miles and Melanie provide online information products, meditations, and spiritual development courses. They have optimized their system and work process, so that they work separate diversified cash engines—which include the brands Ask-Angels, The Angel Solution and Miles' personal brand, MilesBeckler.com. Today, they are semi-retired and have been traveling since 2013.

But, it wasn't always so easy for them. Miles's father was a blue-collar worker, and Melanie's family also struggled financially. Their real journey started in 2009, when as a young couple, newly married, they graduated from college at the same time and were faced with the economic reality of the subprime crisis. Miles sat on a college loan of almost $50,000, and he was worried about finding employment. Nothing out of the ordinary, but for the Becklers, it was compounded with a traumatic experience. Miles's father had gotten laid off after 33 years of loyal service to the same company —just so that "the company could avoid paying full retirement benefits in the wake of corporate cutbacks and restructuring efforts." Due to this, Miles had a tremendous mistrust of the corporate world. Melanie, too, always knew she didn't want to work at a traditional company. She had always been passionate about controlling her financial destiny.

In this time of financial distress and coping with an uncertain future, they were made strong by meditation. "We meditated for several hours a day during college years—it was the only activity that gave us pleasure and satisfaction in life." They realized that they shared a similar passion: to be in control of their own lives and to do what they loved doing.

Financial Freedom - A Journey

Their first step happened unintentionally. Melanie started a simple blog about her experiences meditating. The response was positive. Her blog readers started sharing her posts. Soon, it snowballed into her fans booking one-on-one consultation sessions with her. Observing the zeal of Melanie's readers, Melanie and Miles became enthused about the prospect of earning by just following their passions and doing what they had loved doing. The couple became co-founders of their first cash-engine: Ask-Angels.com.

Though their early efforts paid off, and Melanie had a full calendar of one-on-one consultations, they soon realized they had hit their first growth barrier. Melanie was drained and exhausted from daily consultations, which gave her very little time to meditate and to seek personal growth. The couple recognized that they needed to evolve beyond a simple cash-for-time model.

First, they settled on a division of labor where Melanie was responsible for creating content and Miles was in charge of overseeing the operation and considering the strategic aspects of their growing business. It was perfect teamwork. Together they developed a powerful skill set that would complement each other extremely well.

Second, they gradually replaced the "cash for time" model with a modern earnings model. After helping hundreds of clients, they began to package pre-made audio products that answered the most common questions faced by their clients, making their engagement with them more time efficient. They expanded this into producing digital media, such as audio files, ebooks and physical products. Their digital output gave them an enormous growth boost, and everything became easier. Through organic traffic, they were able to allocate more financial resources to their marketing budget, which resulted in paid traffic and more sales.

But it didn't stop there. Their initial two-person team expanded, too. They would build a team around them consisting of designers, editors, developers, customer support representatives and more. Their growing team allowed Melanie and Miles to maximize the reach of their content with minimal additional effort.

In the next phase of their growth they would add additional cash engines to their platform—and it wasn't even planned. Indeed, "It came naturally" replies Miles when asked about their various business interests today. For Miles, it was natural to expand into *affiliate marketing* based on their combined experiences growing Ask-Angels.com. It made sense to him to create courses and course material based on his years of training and experience. When you listen to Miles in his YouTube videos, you can instantly recognize his authority on various subjects ranging from creating Facebook ads to developing content marketing strategies that convert. This, in turn, has become a separate cash engine, completely unrelated to Ask-Angels.com. Today, they operate three different, independent business lines that give them maximum risk diversification with an edge most professional money managers don't possess. Whether it is on the matter of financial management, digital marketing or customer service, they both understand their businesses by heart.

The Magic Formula

What started out as a simple blog turned into a powerful financial platform that has a combined seven figures in revenues. They have accomplished all this in an astonishingly short time, and have achieved complete financial independence. It took them four years from the time of their graduation to achieving financial freedom and the freedom to design their lives around their own priorities.

What is most astounding Miles paid off his student loans of nearly $50,000 in the same period. Once his loans were repaid it would free up even more cash they would reinvest. How did they do all this in record time?

The answer is as simple as it is logical. High returns on invested capital, high reinvestment rates, and bootstrapping of something they they were experts in. They spent less than $100 on a Wordpress site and initially focused on selling services which quickly achieved cash inflows. Right from the start their margins have been phenomenal. "In the information business we are often seeing 90% to 95% margins on our product sales, which is massive compared to retail, drop shipping or even affiliate marketing" notes Miles.

They also, reinvested most of their earnings on a monthly basis, thus creating a powerful compounding effect—something made possible because they were used to living frugally. Every time they reinvested their savings back into their cash engine, they made sure the investment was profitable. Nothing was left to chance; they paid attention to detail and listened to their client's feedback.

Becoming Intelligent Investors

The Becklers are some of the best investors out there. They are individual investors who have far outperformed any professional money manager. Their annualized returns on invested capital, as measured from 2009 to 2017, were consistently in the *hundreds of percents*. Combined with consistently high savings and reinvestment rates, they have achieved financial freedom in a record time.

Financial experts would argue that they achieved this by taking enormous risks and primitive concentration. I would disagree, as Melanie and Miles never took unnecessary risks or overly hazardous gambles. They made positive asymmetric bets, and it paid out. They took chances by being proactive, but all their financial commitments were carefully assessed before they committed. It fact, both are extremely risk averse and conservative in managing their finances. It was always important for them to build an emergency fund as soon as they were able to put money aside. Today, they both contribute to Social Security, pay into a life insurance plan, and make use of 401(k) plans where they own a combination of low-fee index funds. They consider these measures to be a financial last resort, and participate primarily make use of some of the financial incentives the US government provides.

But that is not their primary form of earnings. Far from it. Their earnings power, their wealth, and understanding of financial freedom come from the investments they made early on. The core of their wealth still stems from their cash-engine platform that has been growing at phenomenal rates since 2009 and produced cash month after month.

It's obvious that the high rates of past returns cannot continue going forward. Since their achieved financial freedom they have been diversifying into more traditional forms of investing. In the process, their investment returns will decline over time as their wealth and asset diversification grows. Nevertheless, the early phase of high investment returns with massive profit margins in a few concentrated investments was vital to boost them to the success they enjoy today. More importantly, it trained them to be responsible financial operators and to become better investors in the process. Today, both are avid students of investing. Miles has developed his own investment approach and Melanie looks out for new opportunities.

What might be most surprising is that the Becklers think of retirement in a very different light since they achieved financial freedom. In fact, retirement as a concept of "ceasing to work" is so foreign to them it lost all meaning. Miles and Melanie travel the world while growing their cash engine platform. They spend time with family and friends while appreciating the things that the world has to offer. Both keep a mindset to be active beyond retirement age, and both pursue interests they consider fulfilling and worthwhile. Why should they change anything if they already lead the lifestyles they envisioned for themselves when they graduated from college in 2009?

TRAVIS JAMISON

Travis Jamison is full of contradictions. He is a super nerd, when it comes to all things related to SEO, web traffic or Amazon's growing competitive advantage, and he's also insanely fit. He is a millionaire several times over, yet he still dresses in H&M V-necks and jeans. He looks like a typical millennial, with his smart phone and sunglasses, and shows all the signs of becoming a great capital allocator and investor at age 32. A serial entrepreneur, CEO and founder of Supremacy SEO and Moat Ventures, he demonstrates how far you could take the concept of cash-engine platforms through bootstrapping a multitude of cash engines and clever investing.

Jamison started out small. In 2009, he sold dietary supplements online while bartending part-time. These were still early days in e-commerce, and in his own words, he was "really bad" at sales. However, by being persistent in his pursuit of financial freedom (some might say stubborn), he improved and mastered all the skills necessary to make it work. He became an enormous financial success. In his own words, he reached a point where he knew he "would never have to work again." In his own words, he reached a point where he knew he "would never have to work again."

A key breakthrough came when he acquired vital skills that would lead the way in all his future enterprises—learning about internet traffic and how he could optimize it to his advantage. Known as Search Engine Optimization (SEO) or how to optimize your website for traffic generated by search engines such as Google. It's an essential part of modern digital marketing and Jamison truly mastered it as all his clients and even competitors would attest to. He monetized these skills by founding Supremacy SEO a company he still owns and oversees to this day.

Jamison went on to create multiple cash engines without the need of bank loans or outside financing. Each time, he used the *stair step method to bootstrapping* financed through his own cash flow resources from his existing cash engines. His many ventures have ranged from simple e-commerce businesses such as selling supplements on Amazon to highly sophisticated SAAS (Software as a Service) businesses that generate millions in sales with very high profit margins. He made them all profitable, and structured them in a way that required minimum day to day input; and thus, he could lead and focus on new projects that required his attention. That's the beauty of his particular cash engine platform.

All his cash engines might have had different business models, but they were all connected in some way. The clearest connection was that they are all digital businesses linked to his core skill of SEO for increasing traffic and ultimately sales. But, there was more. Like a Russian doll model, where he opened up one doll after another, there was always a new promising business idea lurking that he couldn't resist. It gave him a competitive edge in understanding and operating them. It would give him, in value investing terms, a business "moat," a very particular competitive advantage that would make it very difficult for his competitors to replicate his success or his unique cash-engine platform.

Education of a Capital Allocator

In early 2013, Jamison sold his supplement business, cashing in on the rise of e-commerce and Amazon. It would mark his transformation from serial digital entrepreneur to capital allocator. The goal of capital allocation is to allocate financial resources where they're most needed, so that they can maximize returns for their owners.

He reinvested the money he received from his first sale into his most promising cash engine, a SAAS business that would elevate him to the *two comma club*.[ix] He decided to establish his own service fulfilling his needs and requirements. It was a software tool that helped Amazon sellers rank better in Amazon searches. It helped its users to better understand what Amazon clients were shopping for, and it also made it easier to collect reviews from satisfied shoppers. It was an instant success. It grew so fast that it baffled Jamison. The boost of cash he reinvested, into the SAAS business, accelerated the growth at rates he couldn't have imagined. "It was truly fantastic and unexpected," Jamison comments when looking back.

The competition, including potential investors, noticed him. He was approached by an outside investor, and they made him an offer he felt he couldn't refuse. He sold his business for cash while keeping a temporary management and advisory function under the new ownership. When asked why he sold off his best performing SAAS business, instead of reaping more of the rewards in form of investable cash flows, he stated that he "wasn't as sophisticated an investor as he is today," and that he felt he needed a break. Yet, only a few weeks after receiving his check, he launched a new cash engine initiative. His decision was more psychological than logical. When the money hit his bank account, he realized he never had to work again. As it turned out, it was a vital decision that would ignite "a second life calling."

Over the years he had not only amassed enormous amounts of cash but also a treasure chest of information and experience in the digital business world. He didn't know how to invest the abundance of money, so he did what he had been doing since the launch of his first cash engine in 2009—he studied investing and experimented in a very systematic fashion. He devoured investment books and talked to experienced investors with similar backgrounds in the digital entrepreneur community.

Rather than going on a spending spree or giving his money to private bankers or financial advisors (as many do that quickly

---

[ix] Having an income or net worth that is equal to or greater than $1,000,000. This income or net worth generates a number that requires two commas and therefore puts the person into exclusive status as a high income earner or wealthy individual.

acquire large amounts of money), he decided to be in control of all his investment decisions and to continue on a path where he would enjoy a competitive edge. He chose to build or invest in other entrepreneurs' cash engines, but with a slight twist. He was no longer fixated on managing the day to day operations, and entrusted this function to capable managers.

If you looked at his investment portfolio, you would instantly recognize that only a small fraction of it is invested in conventional investments like stock or mutual funds. A larger part, about 20%, is invested in promising, early-stage, high-risk investments part of professionally invested venture capital syndicates.[x] By far, the largest amount of his net worth is invested in cash-producing digital businesses. They are a collection of high-velocity cash engines that he either built himself or acquired in private transactions. The unifying theme of the businesses is that he completely understands all of them by heart. As a further safety mechanism, or what value investors like to call '*Margin of Safety,*' he is either in full control or can oversee their operations directly - occasionally by sprinkling his "magic fairy dust" from Supremacy SEO to give it some gentle padding.[60] The most amazing feat is that his construct continuously generates cash, which increases his liquidity reserves on a daily basis. You may be amused, but it has already caused some head scratching about what to do with all the excess liquidity. He didn't want to sit on dormant cash, so he established his latest venture Moat.VC. It's mission: To build a deal flow for potential new investments, and to attract like minded investors. Another Russian doll? Where will it lead this time?

If you recognize some strange familiarities, it is because there are. Warren Buffett has been a strong proponent of practicing capital allocation, through controlled deal flows, plenty of cash reserves,

---

[x] A group of individuals with well-connected networks and core understanding of key technologies in Silicon Valley and around the world

and a margin of safety. Similar to Buffett, Jamison moves quickly once he is convinced of a good deal and he is not satisfied with market returns or conventional investing platitudes. Like Buffett, he sees financial risk from a very different angle than *Modern Portfolio Theory* or the volatility of market prices might suggest. In fact, he is not bothered by it, because he has intensively studied the subject. He is debt-free, experiences real cash flows rather than accounting earnings, and he continues to do what he has learned and knows best. To this, add a growing cash reserve that he is ready to make use of at any opportunity. This is what operating from a position of financial strength is supposed to look like. He will never be forced into hasty decisions. And most importantly, he isn't bothered about low returns, complex formulas, or even retirement. Indeed, he has found a new calling which adds to his list of contradiction: Achieving high returns at little risk.

CHAPTER 8
LEVELING UP

If you have several of your own cash engines running, you will most likely reach a point where cash accumulates month after month. This, of course, is a wonderful situation to be in. However, those, in such a situation, are faced with the more daunting challenge of investing wisely. You have officially entered Phase II of your investment journey.

If you followed the standard gospel of investing for retirement and investing in general, you would have instantly come across capital markets, stocks, bonds, mutual funds and other financial products. It is widely accepted, researched, and promoted on all available media channels. We are ingrained with the gospel of modern financial theory and conditioned early on.

The result: excessive over-diversification and a portfolio loaded with low-yielding, and possibly overpriced securities. Products that generate fees for a few, but offer very little in return, and no guarantees given. Read the small print. Worse, during this stage of over-diversification and familiarizing yourself with a topic as complex and vast as the study of financial markets and its numerous products offerings, the real money blunders are made. Keen customers clamor for the opportunity to invest, and one place welcomes them with open hands. It's open 24 hours a day, almost six days a week—Wall Street. This is where the biggest and most painful losses are experienced; where prudent investing degenerates into speculation and gambling; and where there's an endless chase of hot tips and easy short cuts.

Unfortunately, most become easy targets for less honest people who have more experience and knowledge about how the game is played. Benjamin Graham, the intellectual forefather of Security Analysis and Value Investing, made the same observation almost 80 years ago, in his masterpiece *The Intelligent Investor*. He wrote:

> "It is amazing to see how many capable businessmen try to operate in Wall Street with complete disregard of all the sound principles through which they have gained success in their own undertakings."[61]

From my own experience, the constant psychological pressure to do something with the money leaves an indelible mark. In this chapter, I will discuss the basics of Wall Street investing and discuss how the game is played; how you should approach financial market investing; and how you can make most of the advantages you possess by default. If you understand some principles and follow some simple rules, global financial markets can be your oyster, and investing for retirement need never be a challenge again.

Operating from a Position of Strength

At some stage in your financial investing journey, it is prudent to consider the purchase of conventional financial products, such as life insurance and additional health, and dental insurance. Having a base 401(k) plan might make sense in well-rounded strategy.

"Wait!" I hear you cry. "Didn't you spend half the book saying that 401(k)s were *bad?*" Well, yes, and I stand by it - *if a 401(k) is all you have.* With leveling up, though, we're proceeding on the assumption that you have cash engines ticking along nicely. In the grand scheme of things in your cash-engine empire, these monthly premiums only constitute a tiny portion of your cash engine revenues. Your main wealth and future growth still come from your cash-engine platform.

It gets problematic when the general Wall Street credo is adopted by accepting lower returns for the benefit of perceived diversification while piling up more and more negative asymmetric bets. As of this writing, the prototypical negative asymmetric bet are index funds, and their close cousins are giant mutual funds.[xi] To escape the sirens of Wall Street and their calls to buy those financial products that are en vogue, I strongly advise that you take a different approach, tailor-made for those with existing cash engine platforms - develop an "edge," and leave as little to chance and wishful thinking as possible.

The Definition of an Edge

On Wall Street, you always want to operate on a basis of financial strength. You never want to be forced to sell and you never want to experience unforced errors, which, like in tennis, are "entirely a result of the player's own blunder and not because of the opponent's skill or effort."[62]

So how can you do this? Well, keep a few things in mind. Just because the price of something went up in the past does not mean you have an edge. Just because a professional recommends a hot stock tip, does not mean you have an edge. Just because you diversify your portfolio into an unrecognizable pie chart with more slices than a real pizza, does not mean you have an edge. A real edge means, you have a higher probability of success for a bet to pay out. There are only three possible ways to achieve a real edge.

1. You get in early and sell when interest is rising: the *"First in, first out"* approach.
2. You make use of great market inefficiencies that includes structural flaws and mistakes committed by others: the *Opportunistic Approach*.
3. You cheat and lie and get yourself an unfair edge. *"Black Edge."*[63]

[xi] I recommend reading my book *Index Funds & ETFs* to understand the argument behind this statement.

But how can you go about acquiring these skills and gain your own edge? There are two simple approaches to finding outstanding opportunities to deploy dormant cash on Wall Street:

1. Continuously search for ideas and mispriced bets in markets and financial assets worldwide.
2. Wait until the markets offer you opportunities within your existing area of expertise.

Both are valid strategies and have their place among established and experienced investors. Many investors combine them. Full-time and professional investors favor the first approach. However, it is extremely time-consuming and requires advanced analytical skills and a strong work ethic. The effort does pay off, because a few talented and experienced investors find appropriate investment opportunities in almost all market conditions - the real "Masters of the Universe." However, there is one weakness; practitioners regularly overestimate their skills at finding opportunities. In the end, most underperform because their financial blunders eat up all their previous gains. As famed author James Rickard noted in *The Road to Ruin:* "superior analytical skill is extremely rare." I don't recommend this approach to the average retail investor, especially those who operate their own cash engines or have everyday jobs. There is not enough time to commit the required level of education and exploration that this approach would require and the outcomes are occasionally nerve-racking.

The second approach is much less work-intensive but has very powerful payouts. You can focus on your primary cash engine—job or businesses—where you utilize your personal competitive edge and enjoy an information advantage. Of course, this only works if you:

• Know in advance what you want to invest in.

- Obtain a purchase price that makes economic sense—i.e. you get a good deal.

Hence, the real essence of your personal edge is not your superior analytical skills, but the anticipation of mistakes by others. This is called the opportunistic approach or, as I like to call it, *the 80/20 investing approach.*

The 80/20 Investing Approach

Pareto's Principle, also known as the 80/20 rule, demonstrates that only a minority of causes lead to the majority of results. Only a few factors contribute to extraordinary investment success. Studying these factors will greatly reduce your workload in the investing process, and at the same time, increase your potential performance and chances for success. So, what are these factors?

In investing, there are times to take bets, and times to stay away. It all depends on your capacity for assessing the odds for each bet, how much you are willing to pay, and how much you are getting in return. In his article "Rich Man, Poor Man," Richard Russell described it as thus:

> "…When bonds are cheap and bond yields are irresistibly high, he buys bonds. When stocks are on the bargain table and stock yields are attractive, he buys stocks. When real estate is a great value, he buys real estate. When great art or fine jewelry or gold is on the "give away" table, he buys art or diamonds or gold. In other words, the wealthy investor puts his money where the great values are."[64]

In this approach, you simply make use of opportunities that financial markets offer you. There is one edge we all enjoy as individual players—the freedom to pick the time and place of our bets. In other words, we can wait for something that interests us at the right price. If nothing else is available, we have the option to say, "No, thank you," and wait.

So, what does this mean in practical terms? Let's use Craigslist as an example, though we could use eBay, Amazon or any good old fashioned flea market and estate auction. (In case you don't know, Craigslist is a website for people selling and buying goods in private transactions.) Every visitor of Craigslist knows that great shopping opportunities can be found on this site. There is also a lot of junk and items at ridiculously high prices that could be bought new on Amazon for a better price; there are also many people who want to scam you outright. So, how do Craigslist shoppers determine what's the fair value of each item?

Well, it depends on their individual interest, experience, and work ethic. Opportunities occur all year long. All experienced Craigslist shoppers know, especially with changing seasons, one may find bargains in different product categories. You might find great snowboards or winter equipment in the spring and summer or coolers and electric fans during autumn and winter. They also know that if people have to move or leave the country, sellers are willing to sell at lower than market prices due to the time pressure to sell their goods quickly. Experienced Craigslist shoppers are experts in a few product categories. For example, they know everything about iPhones or certain appliances. Many female Craigslist pros are experts in luxury handbags and other fashion accessories. When they see something within the category they are experts in, they can instantly determine a fair price and what they are willing to pay for it. This gift is not genetic. Ask any expert in a particular subject, it takes many months, even years, to get to a level of expertise. But for those who love what they're doing, time is relative.

The beauty of buying on Craigslist is that hobby shoppers never have pressure to buy anything from the site. If there is nothing of interest, buyers leave the site and visit another time. If they find something that grabs their attention, and the price is right, they take action and contact the seller immediately.

The financial markets are not very different from Craigslist, garage sales, or flea markets. Buyers and sellers come together to discuss the matter of price on all sorts of goods, products and services. There are always great informational inefficiencies. However, whereas Craigslist's sellers and buyers seem to know that prices are determined by real values, financial market prices seem very often to be determined by popularity or the social impulse to imitate the behavior of others. This is sometimes referred to as "the madness of crowds." Behavioral economists call it "fatal cognitive bias."

For enlightened investors, financial markets offer the same advantages that Craigslist does for hobby shoppers. *There is never a fundamental necessity for you to buy anything from financial markets, whatever your financial adviser, guru, or neighbor might tell you.* Missed opportunities or inflation fears don't matter for a person who has cash coming in every month through their cash-engine platform and who have the luxury of waiting for outstanding opportunities. They know opportunities always come. For financial markets, we all know from experience that great opportunities present themselves like clockwork. Market participants regularly overpay for financial securities, and they panic or are forced to sell. When these opportunities occur, 80/20 investors get active and use their cash.

Always remember, if you have your own cash-engine platform, *only occasionally* should you venture out and consider investments in financial markets or any other asset class. When the odds are in your favor, your edge in place, and you have all the financial resources, then you are on the path to becoming a superior investor.

Recommended Reading

- Richard Russell. "Rich Man, Poor Man," accessed February 28, 2017, http://dowtheoryletters.com/Content_Free/2494.aspx.
- Klarman, Seth A, *Margin of Safety: Risk-Averse Value Investing Strategies for the Thoughtful Investor 1st Edition* (HarperCollins; 1st edition October 1991).

AFTERWORD

We live in a fascinating new world. Lifestyles have changed, and so have the ways you can prepare for retirement. You don't have to listen to the standard gospel of retirement planning, mutual fund investing, and all the other Wall Street nonsense that hasn't worked and most certainly won't work for younger generations. As bestselling author MJ DeMarco describes in *The Millionaire Fastlane*:

> "Go to school, get good grades, graduate, get a good job, invest in the stock market, max-out your 401(k), cut up your credit cards, and clip coupons . . . then someday, when you are, oh, 65 years old, you will be rich."[65]

A more radical interpretation of the old pathway has been given by Mr. Money Mustache:

> "If you save a reasonable percentage of your take-home pay, like 50%, and live on the remaining 50%, you'll be Ready to Rock (aka "financially independent") in a reasonable number of year."[66]

But as founder and semi-retired co-host of the Tropical MBA Dan Andrews noted:

> "Earning a good salary, paying taxes, living life, *all while* saving half of your income—that sounds daunting. And doing it for 17 straight years seems? Even more so."[67]

Simply putting money away is not very efficient; relying on an investment miracle through traditional retirement planning isn't the answer either. We don't have to live like our parents did, and they didn't live like their parents did either. The same counts for how they prepared and invested for retirement as each generation is faced with new financial challenges and economic circumstances. Mr. Money Mustache suggests an extreme path of abstinence, but we don't have to go that route.

The answer, I presented you in this book, is based on the old concept of creating your own cash-generating assets before you buy anyone else's. I call them cash engines in a digital age. They can run parallel, running along at the same time on your personal cash-engine platform, and this creates compounding returns and an exponential growth that Wall Street can only dream of. At the same time, it creates powerful incentives to continuously study and to save and reinvest more. The education value alone is priceless. Once you have plenty of cash coming in month after month, you could focus on purchasing other people's assets, akin to a collector searching for rare and valuable artifacts and looking for bargains. At that stage, return pressure or forced investing will be less of a burden. Single stocks, mutual funds, gold, or real estate are just tokens of a wide field of investment categories and opportunities from which to choose. These are some of the many options that a self-responsible investor could use to his or her advantage.

There is the notion that building cash engines or building cash producing assets is not for anyone. It doesn't have to be. There are so many variations on the cash-engine models described that there is no standard way to choose from what could be rejected by default. I understand that not everyone wants to follow an unconventional path. But then, they should be asking themselves if they are putting their money in stocks and mutual funds in the naive hope that the price will always go up. If you don't have a clue about how it works, you are taking unnecessary risks. These risks can be avoided by staying clear.

In Chapter 5, Cavendish, Melanie and Miles Beckler and Jamison chose a very different path from their parents, because they understood and recognized where those paths would lead. They understood that we are our most valuable asset. They saw financial freedom as a long-term necessity, and they achieved it with no or very little starting capital and by leveraging the only resources abundant to them—time. Through the power of bootstrapping and their determination to succeed they made it work. They established cash engines and cash flows that would power all their future investments.

Did they have to overcome many obstacles? Yes. Was the path to success rocky, lengthy and work-intensive? Certainly. Yet, at very young ages, they all achieved financial freedom, early retirement, and location independence.

My Mission

My self-proclaimed mission is to convince more of you to develop an enlightened view on investing that goes *beyond* Wall Street, mutual funds, and your favorite financial website. I want you to protect yourself from an overhyped and, frankly, corrupt system that exorbitantly rewards the few and punishes many. I want you to be financially self-sustaining and free of an unfavourably skewed system, by continuously studying the topics of entrepreneurship, investing and financial management. Don't aim for the shortcuts of Wall Street!

Today, I have created my own cash engines, e.g. writing books, providing consulting services, and investing in opportunities I enjoy an edge. I will be able to maintain this platform beyond any arbitrary retirement age and any adverse economic cycles. I am not dependent on market prices for my financial future. Yet, I still occasionally trade the markets and make use of financial markets to my benefit. I operate from a basis of financial strength, and I dictate the terms of what I buy or sell and when I do it. I trade when markets offer me outstanding opportunities with much higher return expectations and higher odds of winning, based on my personal edge. I encourage you to also aim for creating something that brings you financial freedom, fulfills you, and endures.

The edge can also be yours.

Accompanying Bonus Material

Sign-up for your account to get access to accompanying bonus material and an exclusive forum where you can discuss and inquire about investing for retirement.

- Here are just a few of the resources that come with membership:
- Accompanying graphs, charts and tables
- Checklists and case studies
- Access to our 8020 Model Portfolio
- Access to an exclusive Facebook group where we discuss investment ideas and recent investment trends
- And more...

To claim your FREE membership go to:

https://www.super8020.com/free-member/

APPENDIX
CASH ENGINE CONCEPT RULES

For your convenience, I have summed up the material into some core rules:

#1 Before you go, do Your Homework

There are a couple of tasks you need to do to make the right financial decisions for yourself. You can read up on these simple tasks in any self-help book on home budgeting and financial management, but here are the basics:

Take an inventory of all your assets. Assessing your earning power and taking an inventory of all your personal assets is vital when it comes investing. You won't be able to avoid unnecessary risk, if you are not sure about your income situation and the financial reserves you have at your disposal. The old adage "nothing ventured, nothing gained" may be true, but doesn't imply that you should be taking dumb risks. Get your financial house in order by measuring and assessing it. Periodically go over these numbers. It will train you to take charge of your financial affairs, which is, ultimately, the single most important step in creating an investment plan.

Check your current and potential earning power, and keep track of expenses. Equally important is the matter of saving to accumulate assets and to build a strong financial base for future investing. Saving works. If there is not enough money for future financial needs such as retirement, you either save more money, work more, work longer, or you create additional earnings opportunities over time, so that you can save more in the future.

Once you have done your homework, you can start contemplating on index fund investing in more detail. It starts with the all-important question: how much money are you willing to lose?

#2 Before you invest in other people's businesses, open a businesses

Warren Buffett, with his usual sagacity, once said, "I am a better investor, because I am a businessman, and a better businessman because I am an investor."

If you study Warren Buffett's early life, you will see how he started out by delivering newspapers, then investing his savings in a pinball machine and a beaten down Rolls Royce that he rented out. He even bought farmland. He created his own business platform based on income-producing assets that would finance all his future endeavors. He admitted that his early experiences of going into his own business taught him valuable lessons for his future career in money management and stock market investing.

Before you even consider buying other people's assets, create your own assets, like Buffett did. Invest in yourself or create a business from scratch. By far the most important income-producing asset will be yourself. Get an education, training and work experience - it will be the best investment you can ever make.

Needless to say, you need to monetize skills and passions. Today, with the diversity of digital platforms, and the reach of the digital world, anyone can bootstrap simple income-producing assets. Your first platform might not turn a profit quickly, but managed well, it will never financially bankrupt you. It would also teach you valuable lessons about business investing, and that can be projected onto financial markets. You would learn the basic concepts of economics firsthand - input and output, as well price determination depending on demand and supply. You would learn the impact of economic cycles on your own business, and how to make it less prone to downturns. You would truly understand the magic of compounding returns that so many financial gurus rave about. You'd experience a crash course of basic accounting and budgeting where you will see money going out, but, initially, little coming in. Automatically, you would learn to control your spending - a vital skill for financial success. You would also understand the difference between real cash flows (i.e. cash hitting your bank accounts vs. accounting earnings).

You would also learn everything about modern marketing and promotional techniques in order to generate sales - how to encourage potential customers to open their wallets for you- from limited time offers to buy one get one free or those dreaded pressure-sales techniques expedia.com is famous for ('50 customers have booked this hotel in the last hour!'). At the very least, you will become aware of these elaborate techniques when they're used on you.

#3 Always assess the odds of success or keep your wallet zipped

Having gone through your personal MBA course, and having your own income-producing assets, you will know how difficult it is to establish and maintain profitable businesses. You will be aware that whenever you open your wallet, by passing your money to someone else, you take substantial risks. Having your own assets will have taught you the skill of assessing the odds of success of each financial transaction. This alone will prevent you from gambling and taking stupid bets in financial markets. You will most likely end up keeping your wallet zipped most of the time.

#4 Compare possible returns in the stock markets with your personal cost of capital

If you established your own cash engine first, and you have your own income-producing assets, you would soon realize that it would be foolish to put the money into the stock markets or any type of mutual fund *all the time*. The reason is you usually get much higher and better returns from the assets you control. Always compare potential returns with the returns you can achieve yourself - at much less risk. Buying index funds, that might make you 5%, but could cost you 50%, will be far less attractive a prospect than investing in your own business where you could make double-digit returns. Ever wondered why top traders and investment managers are so eager to share their tips in expensive research and educational courses or why they are so eager to manage your money? Well, they know that *doing this is a very profitable business* that generates far better returns *than actually following the investment advice and tips they give.*

#5 Avoid overpaying for other people's assets

The biggest risk in investing in financial markets is not price volatility but overpayment risk. Overpayment risk is simply to pay too much for the value you receive in return, i.e. you get much less than previously anticipated. It's common sense to ask for at least equal value for the price you paid. Having your own income-generating asset would train you for this. Overpaying happens in public markets day in and day out. You always pay the price for popularity, and the result is mediocre returns or losses.

#6 Let diversification come naturally

Risk management involves assessing the odds of success with each financial transaction. Today, there is an overemphasis on diversification: people arguing the need to hold 500 stocks, or thousands of stocks, with hundreds of bonds and several funds spread over several asset classes at all times. This is what I like to call "dumb diversification," and it has its limitations. What you end up with is excessive diversification and meager returns at a high fee. Any form of risk management costs money, even if you use cheap index funds.

Investing by definition means taking chances on the future. We cannot completely eliminate this through diversification. If you are worried about portfolio volatility, you shouldn't invest in financial market instruments, but put your money in high quality fixed income securities.

Alternatively, with establishing your primary cash engine comes the understanding of natural diversification. All future cash flows must come from you primary income stream. Hence, efficient diversification means building several income streams over time that will allow you to withstand any financial shock. You will never be forced to sell any of your assets at subpar prices. Keeping liquid assets, such as cash and gold, is your default diversification plan.

#7 Follow the 80/20 way to investing

Financial success relies on only a few decisions. We are our best cash generators. So, we should take care of ourselves first and our own business endeavors. Aim to simplify and streamline your investment strategy and portfolios.

By focusing only on the tasks and decisions that count in your life, you would naturally become more selective with your investments and how you spend time on them. A consequence of this attitude associate with the right people. Actively search for mentors to guide you and even consider becoming an apprentice, as Taylor Person so impressively illustrates in his book *"The End of Jobs."* Team up with others, including your spouse and become partner. Whether you take the role of a junior or senior partner does not matter much. You need to be able to play both roles. In the end, the common goal for all is financial freedom.

CASH ENGINE INSPIRATION

If you recall the three case studies mentioned in this book, you might recognize some commonalities. They might have had completely different social and personality backgrounds, but all three never thought about the traditional sense of retirement planning or financial success and its common side effects. Here are some of the traits all three examples share.

1. They had the right mindset and they took action early
2. They learned from their mistakes
3. They achieved gains far outpacing any returns a traditional way to retirement could offer.
4. None had formal training in investment management or finance.
5. All three focused on steps with limited financial risks, instead of enormous financial gambles - evolution, instead of revolution.
6. They took concentrated bets with limited downside risks but the possibility of very high payouts.
7. They achieved financial freedom in record time through a combination of very high compounding returns, high reinvestment ratios and a focus on cash flows (earnings income) rather than speculating on easy capital gains.

CASH ENGINE CHEAT SHEET

Advantages:

- This model is being tested and proven during a working lifetime not at the very end.
- Its timeless and beyond season
- No discrimination whatsoever
- Much higher compound returns and less financial risk
- Better savings rates - thanks to real incentives
- More tangible and much higher educational value
- Less exposure to the risks of cognitive biases
- More efficient risk diversification
- More satisfaction and true fulfillment

Instructions:

1. Work on you first - your primary source of income
2. Learn, study, and practice the most valuable skillset and expand your network
3. Gradually diversify into additional cash engines
4. Establish a Financial Cushion and continue compounding your money
5. Grow and maintain your cash engines or sell them at favorable prices
6. Make use of capital markets (Stock markets)

CASH ENGINE
STOCK MARKET APPROACH

- Establish your primary financial base first, which can be traditional employment, self-employment or own business. Save and reinvest in your own cash engines with a particular focus on regular income. It's vital to do this before you consider stock market returns. Your default position is to accumulate cash until the markets offer you outstanding opportunities. Try to get some interest on your dormant cash by using safe short-term securities like CDs or fixed deposits.

- Have a passive approach to finding investing ideas by monitoring your own job or business environment and the four additional idea categories (magic categories) I describe in my book The 80/20 Investor. Read your newspaper headlines or listen to what people are talking about.

- Use a checklist. Once you recognize an opportunity, use your own checklist and go through each point with a clear and calm mind. Assessing overpayment risks and getting a clear sense of the opportunity is the highest priority.

- Act with confidence. Once you have made a decision, act decisively. Have confidence and determination when you buy. Commit the majority of your savings in an appropriate "step-in" plan. Once a position is completed, continue saving cash and replenish your cash portfolio for your next investments.

- Don't buy anything if you can't find anything. If you don't recognize no-brainers, wait, continue accumulating cash, read, research, and enjoy yourself. Don't let yourself get fooled or pressured by others, especially professional sales people.

- Rarely sell and accumulate cash for your next purchase. Become a collector of cash engines and quality assets that you never need to sell. If you feel really uncomfortable with your investment, sell and move on. Use a step-out selling plan.

- Concentrate and focus your resources. The main performance comes from being heavily invested in a few rare super bargains - no-brainers. Successful investors put emphasis on quality and fewer investment decisions; they also make much bigger commitments using all cash portfolio resources. The resulting performance is phenomenal. Remember that your cash portfolio will always replenish itself from your primary cash engine, so diversification will happen naturally.

- Get your emotions under control. Practice self-awareness and have a protective mechanism in place. Again, make use of your checklist and develop the mindset of an independent investor who doesn't need the markets and who has all the money coming in from other sources.

ABOUT THE AUTHOR

DAVID SCHNEIDER is the author of the bestselling book The 80/20 Investor on Amazon in Wealth Management, David Schneider bought his first stock in 1994 at age 18. Subsequently, he trained as a commercial banker in Germany and studied finance at London Metropolitan University. He concurrently worked as an Asset Management Trainee and continued as an Equity Research Associate in Tokyo, Japan, where he also studied at Waseda University School of Commerce. From 2005, he co-founded two hedge funds with a Long/Short Equities strategy working in Tokyo and Singapore. He developed his bottom-up value approach for selecting investment opportunities and managing concentrated portfolios based on the 80/20 principle.

Since 2011 David has been an independent investor, entrepreneur, and writer. On his research blog and financial podcast he covers topics including wealth management, financial markets and investment opportunities around the world.

Get in Touch

Twitter: https://twitter.com/WooSchneider

LinkedIn: https://jp.linkedin.com/in/WooSchneider

Schneider R&I: http://www.schneiderai.com/

MORE FROM THE AUTHOR

INDEX FUNDS & ETFS:
What they are and how to use them

Index Funds and ETFs have seen stratospheric growth since the collapse of 2008—benefitting from computerized trading and quantitative forms of investment management. No matter where you look, the gospel of index fund investing has been taken to heart by the media, and the masses, alike. But what is the truth? How exactly do index funds work? Are they really the sure bet they're made out to be? This book will offer a different perspective—one that takes into account the history, structuring, and theorizing behind index funds and ETFs, and lay bare the inner working of the industry.

THE 80/20 INVESTOR
Investing in an Uncertain and Complex World

"Are you ready to set yourself free?" The 80/20 Investor, harnessing the power of the 80/20 principle, simplifies investing. In no time, you will learn where to look for "no-brainer" opportunities, find out how to finance your investment opportunities and minimize risks. This book allows you enter the seemingly intimidating world of investing, with valuable tips from some of those who have changed the game—the Rothschilds, Hetty Green, J. Paul Getty, Henry Singleton, and others. Only with financial freedom can you live the life you want to lead. Let The 80/20 Investor show you the way.

MODERN INVESTING
Gambling in Disguise

Modern Investing is an indispensable guide to becoming an independent investor, rather than giving in to forces that regularly turn us into gamblers or speculators. It will cover the basics every investor needs to know to start a successful investment career free of manipulation and dependence on "experts." By understanding investment history and its core principles, and contrasting it to the gambling culture of today, predominant financial scams and the peculiarities of our financial-political complex, you will be able to draw your own conclusions. More importantly, you will realize what options you still possess to make logical and independent decisions. With the knowledge garnered from this book, you will be able to avoid scams and Wall Street chicanery; and most importantly, you will be able to establish a base investment strategy that can outperform any professional money manager, without the conventional risks. Buy this book and become an independent investor.

GLOSSARY

Affiliate Marketing: A marketing arrangement by which an online retailer pays commission to an external website for traffic or sales generated from its referrals.

Assets Under Management (AUM): Is the total market value of assets that an investment company or financial institution manages on behalf of investors.

Cash Engine: An engine that produces cash non-stop as long as it runs. Anybody can earn money, and if you end up spending less than you make, you have a positive cash flow. You are yourself your primary cash engine—take good care of it.

Chapter 11 bankruptcy: A form of controlled bankruptcy. "This chapter of the Bankruptcy Code generally provides for reorganization, usually involving a corporation or partnership."

Compound Annual Growth Rate (CAGR): The compound annual growth rate is the mean annual growth rate of an investment over a specified period of time longer than one year.

Compound Return: Is the rate of return, usually expressed as a percentage, that represents the cumulative effect that a series of gains or losses have on an original amount of capital over a period of time.

Flash Crash: The quick drop and recovery in securities prices usually caused by computer glitches, flawed programming or order manipulation.

Financial Leverage: Refers to the use of debt to acquire additional assets. A lot of traders borrow money to magnify small speculation gains.

Fund of Funds (FOF): Funds that invest in other funds managed by other companies or different fund managers. It not only spreads the risk of each diversified fund but also among different fund strategies or asset classes. Of course, all this risk diversification comes at a price in the form of another layer of management fees for the managers of the Fund of Funds.

Greater Fool Theory: "The price of an object is determined not by its intrinsic value, but rather by irrational beliefs and expectations of market participants. A price can be justified by a rational buyer under the belief that another party is willing to pay an even higher price."

Index Funds: Index funds are mutual funds—just at low cost. All mutual funds are pools of money managed by professionals and overseen by state law that give you the right to participate in any value increase or decline. Your losses are technically limited to what you paid, but there are no return promises or guarantees.

Magic Categories: Areas 80/20 investors prefer to search for investment opportunities, in order to reduce the workload and achieve above average returns.

Margin of Safety: The original definition of margin of safety is essentially the gap between price and value. Perceived value by an investor can be made up by adding all tangible assets at market price, plus any intangible assets such as licences, brand value, and, most important of all, anticipated growth value. Growth, like anything else, can be priced by investors and is therefore part of valuing an investment.

In more modern interpretations, a margin of safety not only constitutes the price differential between the perceived value and market price, but any additional safety that could support the valuation of an investment. For example, with additional dividend payments, the possibility of a government intervention in a strategic industry, such as banks, oil, or arms production can add to a safety margin. In the case of an index fund, the government or central bank itself.

Market Capitalization: Is the market value of a listed company derived from multiplying its total number of shares outstanding with the current market price.

Matching Contributions: In practice, a certain percentage of each employee's paycheck is set aside, before taxes are deducted, and contributed. If you are lucky, your employer might contribute an additional amount into the employee's plan with each paycheck—known as matching contributions.

Modern Portfolio Theory: Modern portfolio theory (MPT), or mean-variance analysis, is a theory how to construct portfolios on mathematical parameters alone. The goal is to optimize expected return for a given level of risk based on historic price data. Economist Harry Markowitz introduced MPT in a 1952 essay, published in the Journal of Finance. He would later be awarded a Nobel Prize in economics.

Optionality of Cash: Is a permanent option that holder's of cash possess, to either keep cash or to invests it in any asset class, within any industry at any time of the holder's liking and personal preference. Institutional investors including most hedge funds and private equity funds don't have that option.

Overpayment Risk: The most important risk definition for retail investors. It is the risk of paying too much for an investment target than the real value you receive in return. Overpayment usually leads to deferred losses.

Side Hustle: "Is a product or service that you offer or sell on the side of your current full time job to earn extra income on the side." Establishing Cash Engines while you work. Investing the only free resource you have available—Time.

Software as a Service (SAAS): "Is a software distribution model in which a third-party provider hosts applications and makes them available to customers over the Internet."

Trinity Study: An informal name used to refer to an influential 1998 paper by three professors of finance at Trinity University.[1] It is one of a category of studies that attempt to determine "safe withdrawal rates."

Two Comma Club: Having an income or net worth that is equal to or greater than $1,000,000. This income or net worth generates a number that requires two commas and therefore puts the person into exclusive status as a high income earner or wealthy individual.

Ultra High Net Worth Individuals (UHNWI): A person with investable assets of at least US$30 million, excluding personal assets and property such as one's primary residence, collectibles, and consumer durables. UHNWIs comprise the richest people in the world and control a disproportionate amount of global wealth.

Notes

[1] Ask Altucher Ep 309: The End of Jobs, accessed July 2017.

[2] Wikipedia. Pension Definition. https://en.wikipedia.org/wiki/Pension.

[3] CalPERS. https://www.calpers.ca.gov.

[4] Matthews, Chris. California's Pension Funding Crisis Just Got Worse. July 20, 2016. http://fortune.com/2016/07/19/pension-underfunded.

[5] Birdthistle, William A. *Empire of the Fund: The Way We Save Now.* (Oxford University Press).

[6] Prof. Blake, David. Annuities in Pension Plans. World Bank Annuities Workshop 7-8 June 1999.

[7] http://www.economist.com/node/13900145 - The end of retirement – The Economist

[8] Andrew M. Duehren and Daphne C. Thompson, Harvard Loses Almost $2 Billion in Endowment Value, accessed July 2017, http://www.thecrimson.com/article/2016/9/23/hmc-returns-2016.

[9] Employee Benefits Research Institute. https://www.ebri.org/

[10] Birdthistle

[11] Birdthistle

[12] Breslow, Jason M. John Bogle: The "Train Wreck" Awaiting American Retirement. http://www.pbs.org/wgbh/frontline/article/john-bogle-the-train-wreck-awaiting-american-retirement/

[13] Bernstein, William J. *If You Can: How Millennials Can Get Rich Slowly.* (Efficient Frontier Publications).

[14] Robbins, Tony. *MONEY Master the Game: 7 Simple Steps to Financial Freedom.* (Simon and Schuster. Kindle Edition).

[15] Robbins, MONEY

[16] Ferriss, Timothy. *The 4-Hour Workweek: Escape 9-5, Live Anywhere, and Join the New Rich* (Hardcover Harmony; Exp Upd edition December 15, 2009).

[17] Birdthistle

[18] Frankel, Matthew. Here's the Average American's Savings Rate. Accessed September 2016. https://www.fool.com/saving/2016/10/03/heres-the-average-americans-savings-rate.aspx.

[19] University of Oxford. New study shows nearly half of US jobs at risk of computerisation. http://www.eng.ox.ac.uk/about/news/new-study-shows-nearly-half-of-us-jobs-at-risk-of-computerisation

[20] Hawking, Stephen. This is the most dangerous time for our planet. 2016. https://www.theguardian.com/commentisfree/2016/dec/01/stephen-hawking-dangerous-time-planet-inequalityThis is the most dangerous time for our planet

[21] Robbins, MONEY.

[22] Ellis, Charles D. *The Index Revolution: Why Investors Should Join It Now.* (Hoboken: Wiley, 2016)

[23] Robbins, Tony. *Unshakeable: Your Financial Freedom Playbook.* (Simon & Schuster).

[24] Rayner, Gordon. Adolf Merckle: what made this German billionaire commit suicide? Accessed July 2017. http://www.telegraph.co.uk/finance/recession/4210246/Adolf-Merckle-what-made-this-German-billionaire-commit-suicide.html

[25] Richard H. Thaler. *Misbehaving: The Making of Behavioral Economics*. (W. W. Norton & Company).

[26] Greater Fool Theory - Definition. http://www.508fi.org/learn/greater-fool-theory

[27] Birdthistle.

[28] Braham, Lewis. *The House that Bogle Built: How John Bogle and Vanguard Reinvented the Mutual Fund Industry*. (New York: McGraw-Hill Education, 2011)

[29] BlackRock Investor Relations. http://ir.blackrock.com/

[30] Robbins. MONEY

[31] Kane, Libby. A choice you make for your money today could cost you as much as $100,000 by the time you retire. http://www.businessinsider.com/impact-of-fees-on-retirement-savings-2015-7.

[32] Gilchrist, Karen. It's a 'scary' time with a global crisis on the way, LVMH CEO says. https://www.cnbc.com/2017/06/15/be-careful-a-global-crisis-is-coming-says-lvmh-ceo.html.

[33] Melloy, John. Jack Bogle believes the stock market will return only 4% annually over the next decade. 2017. http://www.cnbc.com/2017/03/22/jack-bogle-believes-the-stock-market-will-return-only-4-annually-over-the-next-decade.html.

[34] Bogle John. The Little Book of Common Sense Investing. Wiley (March 5, 2007).

[35] Friedman, Thomas L. It's a 401(k) World. Accessed July 2017. http://www.nytimes.com/2013/05/01/opinion/friedman-its-a-401k-world.html?mcubz=0.

[36] The Economist. The End of Retirement. Accessed July 2017. http://www.economist.com/node/13900145.

[37] The Economist. The End of Retirement. 2009. Accessed July 2017. http://www.economist.com/node/13900145

[38] Thrift Savings Plan, Financial Statements, Dec. 31, 2013, at www.tsp.gov/PDF/formspubs/financial-stmt.pdf.

[39] "The Systemic Plight of Labor," 2013.

[40] Elkins. Kathleens. Self-made millionaire: Don't put money in your 401(k). Accessed July 2017. https://www.cnbc.com/2016/10/26/self-made-millionaire-dont-put-money-in-your-401k.html.

[41] Life Insurance, a Consumer's Handbook/ Belth 2nd ed p23.

[42] Mr. Money Mustache. The Shockingly Simple Math Behind Early Retirement. Accessed July 2017. http://www.mrmoneymustache.com/2012/01/13/the-shockingly-simple-math-behind-early-retirement.

[43] TreasuryDirect. Treasury Inflation-Protected Securities (TIPS) https://www.treasurydirect.gov/indiv/products/prod_tips_glance.htm.

44 Wisner, Matthew. Investing in Gold: You Can't Hack it, Erase it or Delete it. 2016http://www.foxbusiness.com/markets/2016/04/05/investing-in-gold-cant-hack-it-erase-it-or-delete-it.html

45 Thaler, Richard H. Sunstein, Cass R. *Nudge: Improving Decisions About Health, Wealth, and Happiness* (Penguin Books; Revised & Expanded edition February 24, 2009).

[46] Singapore Business Review. Chart of the Day. Accessed July 2017.

http://sbr.com.sg/hr-education/news/chart-day-singapore-has-one-highest-savings-rate-in-world.
[47] Elkins, Kathleen. Here's how much money you should have saved at every age. Accessed July 2017. http://www.cnbc.com/2017/02/22/heres-how-much-money-you-should-have-saved-at-every-age.html.
[48] Andrews, Dan. The Cult of Early Retirement Meets (Or Strangely, Doesn't Meet) The Cult of Entrepreneurship. Accessed July 2017. http://www.tropicalmba.com/the-cult-of-early-retirement-meets-or-strangely-doesnt-meet-the-cult-of-entrepreneurship.
[49] *Futurama*, season 4, episode 8, 'Crimes of the Hot'. dir. Peter Avanzino. Fox, 2002
[50] Nomdadtopia. FAQ: What Is Location Independence? Accessed July 2017. http://www.nomadtopia.com/faq-what-is-location-independence.
[51] Adams, Scott. How to Fail at Almost Everything and Still Win Big: Kind of the Story of My Life. (Penguin Books Ltd. Kindle Edition).
[52] Just 8 men own same wealth as half the world according to Oxfam International. Accessed July 2017 https://www.oxfam.org/en/pressroom/pressreleases/2017-01-16/just-8-men-own-same-wealth-half-world.
[53] Berkshire Hathaway, Annual Letter to Investors 1990.
[54] For more detailed instructions and background information please consult the recommended reading list at the end of this chapter.

[55] Royas, Javier, The art of the bootstrap, accessed July 2017. https://venturebeat.com/2008/11/20/the-art-of-the-bootstrap.
[56] Merriam Webster, Compound Rate, accessed July 2017 https://www.merriam-webster.com/dictionary/compound%20interest.
[57] Markowitz, Harry. Modern Portfolio Theory 1952
[58] Taleb, Nassim Nicholas. Antifragile: Things That Gain from Disorder. (Random House Trade Paperbacks; Reprint edition January 28, 2014).
[59] Podcast Episode #19 - The 8020 Investing Show http://www.8020investingshow.com/investing-ep019-john-cavendish/
[60] Episode Reference, Travis James The 80/20 Investing Show
[61] Graham, Benjamin, The Intelligent Investor: A Book of Practical Counsel (Harper & Row Publisher 1986 edition).
[62] Merriam-Webster, unforced error, accessed July 2017 https://www.merriam-webster.com/dictionary/unforced%20error.
[63] Kolhatkar, Sheelah. *Black Edge: Inside Information, Dirty Money, and the Quest to Bring Down the Most Wanted Man on Wall Street* (Random House February 7, 2017).
[64] Russell, Richard. "Rich Man, Poor Man." (Accessed February 28, 2017). http://dowtheoryletters.com/Content_Free/2494.aspx.
[65] DeMarco, MJ. *The Millionaire Fastlane: Crack the Code to Wealth and Live Rich for a Lifetime* (Viperion Publishing, Kindle Edition).
[66] Mr. Money Mustache, "The Shockingly Simple Math Behind Early Retirement," accessed July 2017, http://www.mrmoneymustache.com/2012/01/13/the-

shockingly-simple-math-behind-early-retirement.

[67] Andrews, Dan. "The Cult of Early Retirement Meets (Or Strangely, Doesn't Meet) The Cult of Entrepreneurship." Accessed July 2017. http://www.tropicalmba.com/the-cult-of-early-retirement-meets-or-strangely-doesnt-meet-the-cult-of-entrepreneurship/

CPSIA information can be obtained
at www.ICGtesting.com
Printed in the USA
LVHW01s1547111217
559406LV00012B/1354/P

9 781975 633868